ONLY IN AMERICA

The Open Society and Jewish Law

STUDIES IN PROGRESSIVE HALAKHAH
General Editor: Walter Jacob
Solomon B. Freehof Institute of Progressive Halakhah.
www.Jewish-Law-Institute.com

Walter Jacob and Moshe Zemer (eds.) DYNAMIC JEWISH LAW
Progressive Halakhah - Essence and Application

Walter Jacob and Moshe Zemer (eds.) RABBINIC – LAY RELATIONS
IN JEWISH LAW

Walter Jacob and Moshe Zemer (eds.) CONVERSION TO JUDAISM
IN JEWISH LAW - Essays and Responsa

Walter Jacob and Moshe Zemer (eds.) DEATH AND EUTHANASIA
IN JEWISH LAW - Essays and Responsa

Walter Jacob and Moshe Zemer (eds.) THE FETUS AND FERTILITY
IN JEWISH LAW - Essays and Responsa

Walter Jacob and Moshe Zemer (eds.) ISRAEL AND THE DIASPORA
IN JEWISH LAW - Essays and Responsa

Walter Jacob and Moshe Zemer (eds.) AGING AND THE AGED
IN JEWISH LAW - Essays and Responsa

Walter Jacob and Moshe Zemer (eds.) MARRIAGE AND ITS OBSTACLES
IN JEWISH LAW - Essays and Responsa

Walter Jacob and Moshe Zemer (eds.) CRIME AND PUNISHMENT
IN JEWISH LAW - Essays and Responsa

Walter Jacob and Moshe Zemer (eds.) GENDER ISSUES IN JEWISH LAW
Essays and Responsa

Walter Jacob and Moshe Zemer (eds.) RE-EXAMINING JEWISH LAW
Essays and Responsa

Walter Jacob and Moshe Zemer (eds.) THE ENVIRONMENT IN JEWISH LAW
Essays and Responsa

Walter Jacob (ed.) BEYOND THE LETTER OF THE LAW
Essays in Honor of Moshe Zemer

Walter Jacob (ed.) with Moshe Zemer SEXUAL ISSUES IN JEWISH LAW
Essays and Responsa

Walter Jacob (ed.) with Moshe Zemer POVERTY AND TZEDAKAH IN JEWISH LAW
Essays and Responsa

Walter Jacob (ed.) NAPOLEON'S INFLUENCE ON JEWISH LAW
The Sanhedrin of 1807 and its Modern Consequences

ONLY IN AMERICA

The Open Society and Jewish Law

Edited by

Walter Jacob

in association with

Moshe Zemer

Solomon B. Freehof Institute for Progressive Jewish Law
Rodef Shalom Press
Pittsburgh, Pennsylvania

Published by the Rodef Shalom Press
4905 Fifth Avenue
Pittsburgh, Pensylvania
U.S.A.

Copyright © 2009 Solomon B. Freehof Institute of Progressive
Halakhah

Library of Congress-in-publication-data

Jacob, Walter 1930-

Zemer, Moshe 1932-

ISBN 0-929699-21-1

Dedicated

in loving memory to

Daniel Benjamin Jacob

1966-2007

When Time, who steals our years away
Shall steal our pleasures too,
The memory of our past will stay
And half our joys renew

CONTENTS

ACKNOWLEDGMENTS

The Freehof Institute of Progressive *Halakhah* continues to express its gratitute to the Rodef Shalom Congregation for its support of technical matters connected with this volume. Special thanks go to Nancy Berkowitz for her careful copy-editing; she has helped us with many previous volumes and in this major way supported the efforts of the Institute. We remain very grateful to Barbara Goldman for her assistance with portions of the initial typescript.

INTRODUCTION

America has had a greater influence on Jewish life and thought than any other land. America was different from the beginning. Here, we Jews were part of the great democratic experiment with religious freedom. We sought ways of adapting the *halakhah*, the basic expression of Jewish life and thought, to this new found freedom. Was it possible or even necessary to adjust or reinvent the halakhic path? What roles have democracy, personal autonomy, and the absence of authority played in this effort? The interplay of these and other forces has influenced all Jewish life in ways both obvious and subtle.

For the first time in two millennia we Jews live in a land not dominated by a single religion. Jewish life in previous countries with their official religions could be pleasant for centuries as we lived in reasonable harmony with the majority; however, more frequently we were barely tolerated, persecuted or forced to conversion. The Jewish minority was often the only nonconformist group. As the dominant culture did not know what to do with us they gave our communities a semi-autonomous status, kept us more or less isolated and used our existence for whatever political purpose was expedient – sometimes as convenient scapegoats while on other occasions as part of an economic experiment. Whatever the situation, the Jewish community governed itself virtually as a semi-autonomous "statewithin a state" through a well developed system of *halakhah* and even added protective layers to the walls which the majority had built around us.

In America the imposed isolation ceased, we became citizens governed by the national law and the older system of separate status disappeared. As we were no longer a "state within a state" and could now develop our religious life as we wished. Much of the Jewish community seized that opportunity to reinterpret the traditions and to experiment. Reform Judaism was in the forefront. In contrast to nineteenth century Europe it was possible here as the government had no interest in the religious path which we took. Complete freedom to practice as we wished, to change, or remain static was granted. The essays in this book will show how this has taken place.

The American freedom has increased the influence of the surrounding cultures. We felt free to learn from other groups and try new structures, customs, and patterns. Experimentation in every area of life and practice was possible for those who wished it, while others who wanted to isolate themselves within separate enclaves were free to do so.

The essays in this volume look at some aspects of this developing American path and how we continue to use this freedom. The traditional *halakhah*, designed for a different world, has been modified by all segments of the Jewish community. In this country it never became the legal system governing the entire Jewish community with accompanying enforcing powers. Judaism became pluralistic and voluntary for all Jews. These studies are concerned with these developments within the Reform and Liberal Jewish community.

The essays in this volume look at selected issues from a theological, historical or practical context. Leonard Kravitz begins with a theological analysis and discusses where this American freedom has led us. Peter Knobel leads us in a somewhat different direction as he looks at the conflict which has arisen between personal autonomy, *halakhah*, and *mitzvah* – issues which would not have been raised before the Emancipation, but which are very much with us now. My essay looks at the mechanisms of change which we have adopted and their relationship to the traditions of the past. I have illustrated this through the Reform movement's efforts to elevate the status of women, beginning with the Jewish emancipation in Europe and continuing in America. Ruth Langer has used the funeral for her study. Even in this normally very conservative portion of religious life where everyone wishes to adhere to old laws and traditions, the influence of America has been great. The Hebrew essay of Samuel Adler represents the scholarly effort of a German rabbi, who later settled in America, as he sought to root changes in the status and practices of women in the *halakha*h. The essay represent a portion of the vast array of Reform Jewish thought on these and associated questions.

Although each essay investigates one avenue of this development, together they demonstrate how different the American approach to the *halakhah* and Jewish religious thought has become.

AMERICA - JEWISH THEOLOGY AND HALAKHAH

Leonard Kravitz

I begin with a text that all of us know. It is the Hebrew text, which we could sing instantly – *ein kelohenu, ein kadoneinu, ein k'malkeinu,* "There is none like our God, there is none like our Lord, there is none like our King"! For the moment, look at the emotional quality of that one Hebrew word: *ayn* – "No," there, to use a common locution, "ain't," there is no God, there is no other Lord, there is no other King – "none," there is "none" – no, no! Nobody has what we have, no matter what others may think, we've got it, they don't! We've got a God, we've got a Lord, we've got a King! And whatever others think they have, they are wrong! We've got something and more than something, we've got the God, we've got the Lord, we've got the King! To borrow the phrase from "Porgy and Bess," they've got plenty of nothing!

Having sung a song, let us now learn some texts. Look what Jewish tradition teaches about other gods: in the Bible, in Psalm 115, the *Hallel,* we read: "Other gods are idols, the work of men's hands: they have eyes, but they don't see, they have ears, but they don't hear – and those who follow them, (I put in my own parenthetical comment, 'because they are so stupid') will be like them." Indeed, the Torah does mention "other gods" *elohim aherim,* in the Ten Commandments ; but lest you think that there are such things, the *Mekhilta,*[1] tells that there are no other gods, that *aherim* does not mean "others," so that you might think that there are "other gods" but rather the word means that believing in such gods, makes those who do, into *aherim,* different kinds of people, or the word means that belief in such erroneous notions *me-aher,* delays that what such fools hope for, or the word means that to believe in such folly is to *aher,* keep changing, what kind of gods you believe in. Because *peti ya-amin l'khol davar,* "A fool may believe in anything"[2] and such other 'gods' are no things, really nothing, the *Mekilta* further warns us not only not to worship them, but not to mention them or if we can help it, have others not mention them.[3]

Other gods are no things; they are delusions that others may have. We've got a God that is real. What kind of God? Nachmanides reminds us the first word of the Ten Commandments (*aseret hadibrot, "anokhi"*) "I," "its Me" was to proclaim that the God of Israel is a God who knows, who acts, who provides, and whose act of deliverance by the use of miracles provides that God also created the world out of nothing.[4]

That kind of God, a creator God, according to Saadia Gaon (882 – 942) provides proof for the ultimate sanction of Jewish Law, for if you can believe in creation, you can believe in *tehee-yat ha-meitim.*[5]

Thus, our God provides deliverance in this life and perduration and reward in the next. That is why we can sing *ein keloheinu*: our God is real, our God acts unlike the so-called gods of the others! There is none like our God because our God is real and their gods are fake!

Because our God is real, He is our *Adon,* our Lord, our master, and we are His willing servants; we are His *avadim* and we are bound to serve Him – More than that: He is our King and we are His people. His people – and not someone else's People; and others are not His people! We belong to His kingdom, which like other kingdoms occupies a specific place on the globe and has a particular language. In fact, we are singing in His language, in Hebrew. As members of His kingdom, we are bound by his *gezeirot,* His specific commands, for we are bound to do things that others are not bound to do, *davke,* because we are His people and He is our king![6] Thus there is a connection between our concept of God, our self concept and our concept of our task, or to say it another way, there is a linkage between how we understand God and how we understand being a

Jew. Being a Jew means what we do now and what we do so there will be Jews in the future. That relates to certain beliefs and certain behaviors. A crucial belief that motivated those behaviors in the past was that we were doing what God wanted us to do, that the God we believed in could tell us that, could somehow convey to us His will, call it revelation, call it *matan torah*, or call it what we learned from the text of *ein keloheinu.*

What revelation gave to Jews was law: *Torah uMitzvot* were part of the Jewish vocabulary. It also gave the Jew the sense of being special: we learned that we were God's treasure from among all the peoples, a *mamlechet kohanim v'goy kadosh,*[7] we were His treasure and that was why He was our *Adon*, Lord and Master, we were a kingdom of priests and that was He was our King. As that kingdom passed through time, subservient to its King, it would develop *halakhah* as a divinely originated system of law.

And now, having sung a song, having learned some texts, and having reflected on the meaning of the song and the texts, we, as Reform Jews, face a problem. That is suggested by another text, a text that some of us know as well as we know *ein keloheinu,* because it was in the old Union Prayer Book on page 155, the facing page to *ein keloheinu's* on page154. It is not a translation of *ein keloheinu* but is a paraphrase; its opening lines ask a different question than the opening lines of *ein keloheinu;* it asks,
> Who is like Thee, O universal Lord?
> Who dares Thy praise and glory share?

Note well: "Universal Lord!" Not "our God," not "our Lord," not "our King"! "Universal Lord"! Would such a God be interested in a specific people? Would such a God make a covenant with a particular people? One wonders! We are not surprised, therefore, to read the first two lines of the next stanza:
> Thy tender love embraces all mankind,
> As children all by Thee are blessed,

"All mankind" and "children all" – Different! Page 155 has moved far from page 154 of the old Union Prayer Book! And we have moved far from *adoneinu* and *malkeinu!* Those two words, however, occur in English translation in the last stanza of the paraphrase:
Whate'er to us is deepest mystery,
Is clear to Thee, our Lord and King.

Perhaps it is an unconscious bit of irony or perhaps some profound lesson is being taught, a lesson that has so far eluded me, that the words, "deepest mystery" are linked to "Lord and King"! A universal God could not have been the kind of God that motivated *ein keloheinu* nor, indeed, be viewed as "Our Lord and King"! A God in general cannot give a law in particular!

Such a notion of Deity is assumed by the founding theological document of American Reform Judaism, the Pittsburgh Platform. What one is immediately struck by is the nonspecificity of its theological language, from descriptions of texts held to be sacred to God-language. Reading the first Principle:

> We recognize in every religion an attempt to grasp the Infinite One, and in every book, source or book of revelation held sacred in any religious system the consciousness of the indwelling of God in man.
> We hold that Judaism presents the highest conception of the God-idea as taught in our holy Scriptures and developed and spiritualized by the Jewish teachers in accordance with the moral and philosophical progress of their respective ages. . . .

and the second Principle:

> We recognize in the Bible the record of the consecration of the Jewish People in its mission as the priest of the One God.. . . .

We may note that although the words "book of revelation" (held sacred in any religious system), "holy Scriptures," and "Bible" are mentioned, a word specific to Jews, "Torah," is not.

And though "book of revelation" is mentioned, it might be useful to here reflect on the assumptions of such a term. The notion of revelation carries with it specificities: a specific revealer, a specific person or group, and a specific body of information that was revealed. Polemics between religions were and are based on different understandings of those specificities. One finds that Religion A makes its claim for validity on the basis of Revelation A; nowhere will one find Religion A granting the possibility that Religion B has revelation superior to its own. Religion A may magnanimously grant that the adherents of Religion B may think that they have a revelation, but the adherents of Religion A (and the adherents of Revelation B, were the situation reversed) would maintain that such thinking was erroneous.

The kind of God-idea mentioned in the Pittsburgh Platform did not embrace such specificities. We read of the "Infinite One, God, God-idea, the One God" such terms do not in themselves carry any connection to a particular people nor are they specific to any people. "The indwelling of God in man" apparently occurs to any person and not specifically to a Jewish person. The invocation of "every religion" suggests at least the formal acceptance of other patterns of belief, something that the *Mekhilta* would not have done. One wonders whether in 1885, a minority religious group seeking acceptance into broader society, could have denounced the existence of the various religions of that broader society. "Every religion" suggests an affinity with Judaism, or at least the Judaism of the writers of the Pittsburgh Platform, to the other religions existing side by side in the country. The question of which religion is the right one or which religion came from God is rendered moot by the "indwelling of God in man": all persons, qua person, can have God, indeed, does have God within him or her. It is clear that such a concept of God, a God related to the totality of humankind could not be the kind of God able to provide that revelation claimed by any religious group.

Without that specific revelation, the God within would hardly be interested in those specificities that would make the Jew visible on the outside; hence the third Principle of the Pittsburgh Platform:

> "We recognize in the Mosaic legislation a system of training the Jewish people for its mission during the national life in Palestine, and today we accept as binding only its moral laws and maintain only such ceremonials as elevate and sanctify our lives, but reject all such as are not adapted to the views and habits of modern civilization."

Thus, what the Pittsburgh Platform asked of the Reform Jew of 1885 was essentially the same as that which any other modern religion would ask of its adherents: a commitment to some generalized ethical theory and practice. On the basis of a universal God and a universal demand put upon the Jew, one could wonder how the specificity of Judaism would be maintained. The linkage between the notion of a particular God and a particular people had been broken.

The notion of a "universal" God, a God, as it were, in general, and the theological problems so created did not wait until the modern world. It and its attendant problems already existed in the medieval world, once philosophy entered that world. The philosophers' God was an idea, a simple idea, an unchanging idea, an idea that could be apprehended by any philosophically trained person, but not by one philosophically ignorant. Such an idea is presented in its most succinct form by the philosopher that appears in Halevi's _Kuzari;_ for him, God is an entity.

> Above desire and intention..and . . . He is . . . above the knowledge of individuals, because (they) change . . . whilst there is no change in God's knowledge. He

..does not know thee, much less thy thoughts and actions, nor does he listen to your prayers . . . .[8]

Though God as Idea could not be related to the traditional notion of revelation, it appears in the thought of many of the medieval Jewish philosophers, albeit arrayed in careful disguise.

Thus, Saadia Gaon, (882 – 942) head of the Academy of Sura and compiler of a version of the *siddur*, held that

> Were we..make use only of expressions that are literally true, it would be necessary to desist from speaking of Him as one who that hears and sees and pities and wills to the point that there would be nothing left for us to affirm except the fact of His existence. [9]

So *shomaya tefilah* is not "literally true" – one may wonder, what is it? If all we can say is that God is, and not "sees" and "pities," what do we do with *r'ey onyeinu* or *hus v'racheim aleinu*? If we cannot say that God "wills," how then can we say that God reveals? One wonders what hint Saadi was giving to his reader when he told him the four constitutive elements of the Torah, viz., that we should revere God, that we should not contemn God, that we should not hurt one another, and that we should hire one another are the things that "Reason demands"![10] Upon reflection, one would conclude that what "reason demands" after all, reason, not revelation, must supply!

One might think that one would receive a less problematic viewpoint from Judah Halevi (1080 – 1142) called by some, "The Poet Philosopher." Reading about the Divine Attributes, however, one learns that neither the "creative," nor the "relative," nor the "negative" attributes described God as God is. We learn further that the divine essence is exempt from complexity and divisibility, and "one" only stands to exclude plurality...All these attributes neither touch on the divine essence Nor do they lead us to assume a multiplicity.[11]

(Halevi will immediately discuss those attributes connected to the Tetragrammaton that deal with divine creation without intermediaries. We will learn on the following page, however, that "metaphorically, He is called JHWH who descended on Mount Sinai."[12] What that metaphor means will become clear in the next citation.)

That notion that seems specific to Halevi, that of *inyan elohi*, the Divine Influence, and which in his thinking seems to be the source of revelation, turns out to be as automatic in operation as the philosopher's notion of the Active Intellect[13] and at the end of the book is identified with the Active Intellect.[14] Thus, a God beyond affect, a God-concept of utter simplicity, God as Idea, drives toward a notion of revelation as reason event for Halevi!

Though Maimonides might write that"the fundamental belief in prophecy precedes the belief in the Law. For if there is no prophet, there can be no Law."[15] It is clear that the God in which the Guide presents is a God beyond affect[16] in whom Will, Wisdom and Essence are all one and unchanging.[17] Hence, revelation in terms of prophecy given to a prophet or a people at a specific time and in a specific place would be problematic.

Though most carefully concealed, the notion of revelation becomes the notion of reason in Maimonides' thinking. The reader for whom he wrote would know the Active Intellect was always active.[20] (MN II:12, pp. 279, II:18, pp. 300, II:32, pp. 361); those prepared to receive its input would receive it; and depending on the recipient's physical philosopher or a prophet. The admixture of imagination, for Maimonides, a physical disposition, distinguished the prophet from the philosopher. Though in one place, the Guide described the prophet as "someone perfect to the utmost degree,"[19] the reader will learn that the term "prophet" is amphibolous when applied to Moses and any other prophet[20] and then that reader will be able to deduce the reason why that is so, when he learns that "imagination" did not enter into Moses' prophecy.[21]

Maimonides gives further hints as to the nature of prophecy and what did (or did not) occur at Sinai. The reader learns that when the Torah says that at Sinai "all the people saw the sounds,"[22] what they saw was a vision of prophecy.[23] Later the reader will learn that what happens in such a vision, "are not real actions, actions which exist for the external senses.[24]

The *aseret ha-dibrot* the seeming prime examples of revelation, have an interesting meaning for Maimonides as we learn from his interpretation of a rabbinic dictum;

> They heard "I" and "Thou shalt have" from the mouth of the Force. "They" means that these words reached them just as they reached Moses . . . . For these two principles, (i.e.,) the existence of the Deity and his being one are known by human speculation alone.[25]

What can be learned by human speculation alone, we learn, conveys no superiority to the prophet over anyone else who has learned it.[25] Moreover, we learn something about the remainder of the Decalogue.

> As for the other *commandments*, they belong to the class of generally accepted opinions and those adopted in virtue of tradition, not to the class of intellecta.[27]

(The reader for whom Maimonides wrote would remember that being reduced to the acceptance of "generally accepted opinions" was Adam's punishment for sin[30] and opinions adopted in virtue of a tradition were not sufficientlyworthy to allow entrance in the King's Palace of Maimonides's)in his Parable.[29]

Revelation plays no role in Maimonides' theory of human perfection; according to him,

> to this ultimate perfection there do not belong either actionsor moral qualities and that it consists only of opinions toward which speculation has led and that investigation has rendered compulsory . . . . (It) is the only cause of permanent preservation."[30]

Having understood what Maimonides' hint here, the astute reader will be able to understand the Guide's later hint dealing with the 613 commandments of the Torah: "Thus all (the commandments) are bound up with three things: opinions, moral qualities, and political civic actions."[31]

It is clear then that two-thirds of the commandments of the Torah, i.e., moral qualities and actions, are useless in achieving human perfection and perduration and the only opinions which count are those which are philosophically provable, like the first two statements of the Decalogue.

If the God Idea of these (and other) Jewish philosophers had vitiated the notion of revelation and with that the basis of the Law, why was the Law still observed? How could it not be observed? The social reality trumped whatever ideological changes that might have occurred. What happened to Jews in general overrode what some Jews might have thought in particular. (A process that will recur!) The Jews, throughout the Middle Ages, whether under Christian or Muslim domination, were a separate legal entity, separate by external law and separate by internal law. Whatever any Jewish philosopher might come up with did not affect that reality. Moreover, it could be argued, that the views of the philosophers, so carefully concealed, did not affect the mindset of the majority of the people who were to observe the law. They were not tempted by looking at the views of the others outside the community; those views were encased in a different legal system, so that to accept those views would be to accept the legal system of the surrounding society, a thought faced with abhorrence by those within the society.

The changes in society brought on by the advent of merchant capitalism, the Enlightenment, and the French Revolution were to change the legal systems, internal and external that surrounded the individual Jew. That change would affect both ideas and behavior, what Jews believed and what Jews did. The Jew became, in theory at least, a citizen. Being a citizen meant being a different kind of Jew: no longer under a separate legal system and no longer treated as part of a separate entity by the legal system of the host country. To be a citizen meant: to be just like every other citizen and to view other citizens, the words of the Napoleonic Sanhedrin of 1806 – 1807, as one's "brother."[32] Acceptance of citizenship and with that the end of separate legal status changed, at least in theory, changed who Jews were, as they were seen by themselves and as they were seen by others. M. Portalis, one of Napoleon's commissioners at the Sanhedrin, summed up the theoretical effects of that change in the phrase, "the Jews ceased to be a people and remained only a religion."[33]

To be part of "only a religion" was to be like other faith communities in France: a voluntary association of French citizens, who differed, at least in theory, from one another, by what they did on weekends and a few other days during the year. To be a citizen, to be part of "only a religion" meant to be outside a separate legal system and within the legal system of the general society. To be a citizen meant to be part of a legal system that did not claim divine sanction and that in some cases could override systems that did. To be a citizen of France, for example, might mean going to war against citizens of another country, even if those other citizens were fellow Catholics or

Jews. Whatever *ein kemalkaeinu* had once suggested to the Jew, as part of the Jewish people, now in the new setting of citizen, the Jew got a new king. That new king (or whatever the title of leadership was) was the king or whatever the leader was called of the particular nation of which the Jew was not a citizen.

On a conscious or on an unconscious level, to be a citizen meant to relate to others in a different manner than before, to be allowed to enter the society and concomitantly to allow oneself to enter the broader society. To be a citizen meant, perforce, to view the other differently than one had viewed the other heretofore. Before, one might see in the Hebrew word *goy*, the biblical term for nation that was applied to the non-Jew as a reflection of a prior situation in which the Jew was part of one nation and the non-Jew part of another nation. To be a citizen for the Jew meant to view oneself as part of the same nation as the non-Jew. The nation state would be the marker of identity for both; "religion" as practiced within the new situation of the nation-state would be the marker of separate identity. In theory, the *goy* becomes one's "brother"!

Not only would the *goy* change, but so would God! The old specificity could not apply in the new situation; the "God of the Hebrews" or the "God of the Jews" would perforce become the God of all people, even as the bowdlerized biblical phrase was to be found on the walls of so many Reform Congregations; "My house shall be a house for all people."[34]

The philosophers of the Middle Ages and developers of modern Reform theology faced the same problem, even though their philosophical carriers differed; the God-concept with which they operated could not be related to a theory of revelation. Without revelation, there would not be a way of justifying the panoply of law and commandments; without revelation there could be no halakhic system nor could there be the specifics of separate religious systems; without revelation there could be no justification for the existence of separate religions. A system might be available to any person by virtue of being rational. Without revelation, one might posit a system of "rational" laws, i.e., general ethical systems. Such "rational" laws could not in themselves justify a particular religious system.

If the God-idea of Reform Judaism could not justify revelation and without revelation one could not justify specific law to generate specific behaviors that would justify and maintain the Jewish entity, if Jews were merely a religion like unto other religions, how could one understand the progression from the Pittsburgh Platform to the Columbus Platform to the Centenary Perspective? How could we understand our present interest in *halakhah* if on the one hand there is not theoretical basis for it in the sense of a concept of deity that would drive for it and if on the other hand there is no structural necessity for the kind of separate Jewish law that would make its development in *halakhah* necessary?

Medieval thought does provide a suggestion, if not a definitive answer. It is in the thought of Hasdai Crescas, author of *Ohr Ha-Shem,* the *Light of the Lord.* After the pogroms of 1391, when his only son was murdered by a mob, Crescas, once high in the society as financial adviser to the realm, wrote a philosophical treatise which attacked the assumptions, viz., those of Aristotle, upon which Maimonides and Gersonides had built their philosophical edifices.[35] For our discussion, what Crescas decried is less important than that which he asserted: that the relation between God and person was not intellect as Maimonides and Gersonides had held, but *chesed,* love.[36] God loved the world, God loved people; but most of all, God loved the Jewish people.[36] He manifested that Love by giving that people Torah and *Mitzvot* and that people manifested their love for God by studying that Torah and observing those *mitzvot.*[37]

If we take Crescas as a model, one might say that when a group of people are treated in such a way as to emphasize they are a specific group, a people, not merely an aggregation of individuals, then they may respond with mechanisms that maintain that sense of being part of a people, if they wish to remain within the group or there is no way of leaving the group.

Whatever the theory of citizenship developed in the 19th century, the 20th century suggested that total absorption into the society as just another citizen was not available to Jews, at least in most countries. Totalitarian regimes of various persuasions found common targets in the Jew. If the words, "The Jews have ceased to be a people and are now merely a religion" no longer seemed applicable, if a Jew was no longer seen or no longer saw himself as fellow citizen and thus part of "merely a religion," then Jews, willy nilly, would be resurrected to being a people once again. One might note that Jews in eastern Europe who flocked into America from 1885 to 1923 had, in the main, never lost their sense of ethnic identification, whether or not they maintained a connection to those ideas that had first brought it forth.

Hence the Columbus Platform of 1937 began noting "the changes that have occurred in the modern world" and had as the first part of the statement on "Judaism and its Foundations," the words, "Judaism is the historical experience of the Jewish people." The fifth article within that section, entitled, "Israel" stated that.

> Judaism is the soul of which Israel is the body. Livingin all parts of the world, Israel has been held together by the ties of a common history, and above all, by the heritage of faith. . . . [W]e maintain that is by its religion and for its religion that the Jewish people has lived.[39]

Though the Columbus Platform situated Judaism within the Jewish People and claimed the two were co-extensive, the problem of Jew as citizen still presented itself and thus the Platform had to assert that

In all lands where our people live, they assume and seek to share loyally the full duties and responsibilities of citizenship and create seats of Jewish knowledge and religion.

The Platform also addressed the issue of Zionism that had been a problem for much of the early Reform Judaism:

In the rehabilitation of Palestine, the land hallowed by memories and hopes, we behold the promise of renewed life for many of our brethren. We affirm the obligation of all Jewry to aid in its upbuilding . . . .

So Jews are members of a particular people, linked worldwide by religion, citizens of various countries in which they live and interested in establishing a national life in yet another country. Although these statements may reflect the true nature of that unique entity, the Jew, it is clear that they presented, then, in the time of the Columbus Platform and today certain tensions, tensions acerbated by the blessed fact of the existence of the State of Israel.

When one looks at the initial definition of the nature of Judaism and then at the definition of Israel, one finds the beginning statements are essentially the same in different words; both affirm the existence of a people passing through time developing certain notions that motivate further development. Thus, to read the entry on "God" one finds that

The heart of Judaism and its chief contribution to religion is the doctrine of the One, living God, who rules the world through law and love. In Him all existence has its creative source and mankind its ideal of conduct. Though transcending time and space, He is the indwelling Presence of the world. We worship

Him as the Lord of the universe and as our merciful
Father.

It is clear that such a notion of Deity developed over time and
indeed requires some reflection. That God could be a model of
conduct assumes a certain notion of God selected out from various
Biblical and Rabbinic sources. It is that process of ongoing selection
that stands behind that notion of Torah and revelation in the Platform.
We learn that

> Torah. God reveals Himself not only in the majesty,
> beauty and orderliness of nature, but also in the vision
> and moral   striving of the human spirit. Revelation
> is a continuous process, confined to no one group and
> to no one age.

Revelation that is continuous and open to every one would not
provide specificity for the Jewish group, therefore the Platform had to
continue,

> Yet the people Israel, through its prophets and sages,
> achieved unique insight in the realm of religious truth.
> The Torah, both written and oral, enshrines Israel's
> ever-growing consciousness of God and the moral law.

Revelation, then, is something achieved, not something
received. "Israel's ever-growing consciousness of God and the moral
law" makes it possible to reject certain of the laws of the Torah as not
befitting the present age while holding on to other notions. In a
manner similar to that of those thinkers that wished to combine the
biblical notion of creation with evolution, whatever could be retained
was felt to have some divine imprimatur; whatever was to be sloughed
off would depend on the needs of the age.

Still, the Columbus Platform maintained the connection between Judaism and morality, stating that

> In Judaism religion and morality blend into an indissoluble unity. Seeking God means to strive after holiness, righteousness and goodness. The love of God is incomplete without the love of one's fellow men.

The Centenary Perspective of 1976 reflected on the hundred years that followed the founding of the UAHC in 1873, the founding of the Hebrew Union College in 1875, the Holocaust, and the founding of the State of Israel. It conveys magnificently the tensions of Jewish life, the "this" and yet "that" of Jewish existence. It is a kind of "uncertain trumpet" that reflected the problems of that time and unwittingly predicted some of the problems of our own time. It began with a notion of "Diversity within Unity"; the problem with such a formulation that it becomes difficult to understand what precisely is being said. That problem may be seen at the very beginning with a statement about God

> The affirmation of God has been essential to our people's will to survive. In our struggle through the centuries to preserve our faith we have experienced and conceived God in many ways. The trials of our own time and the challenges of modern culture have made steady belief and clear understanding difficult for some. Nevertheless, we ground our lives, personally and communally on God's reality and remain open to new experiences of the Divine.

To say the least, such a formulation requires further reflection. The difficulty is that the word "God" is not defined. Is God the affirmation of the will to live? The first sentence would suggest that. Is God the "Lord of the universe and merciful Father" of the

Columbus Platform? One suspects that the phrase "the trials of our own time" suggests the perennial problem of evil made even more manifest by the Holocaust! Is "God" so difficult an entity to conceive and define that we can only approach the matter with undefined and indefinable words? One then wonders how the various conceptions of God can be related to the meaning of revelation and an understanding of the role of the Jewish people.

The difficulty of defining God is paralleled in the Centenary Perspective by the difficulty of defining the Jewish people and Judaism. The reason given is:

> Both are in the process of becoming Jews, by birth or conversion, constitute an uncommon union of faith and peoplehood. Born as Hebrews in the ancient Near East, we are bound together like all ethnic groups by language, land, history, culture and institutions. But the people of Israel is unique because of its involvement with God and its resulting perception of the human condition. Throughout its long history, our people have been inseparable from its religion with its messianic hope that humanity will be redeemed.

Here in the description and loose definition of the Jewish people, the problem of the definition of God reemerges. It would be helpful to understand what the term meant in the phrase "involvement with God." Once again, the problem of evil arises.

The problem of the definition of God becomes even more crucial in the discussion of Torah. To read that "Torah results from the relationship between God and the Jewish people." To read further that

> The records of our earliest confrontations are uniquely important to us. Lawgivers and prophets, historians

and poets gave us a heritage whose study is a religious imperative and whose practice is a means to holiness

is to make a number of concealed assumptions about the veracity of the texts, the surety of the transmissions of those texts, and the authors of those texts. What is clear is that Torah is not here understood as the result of revelation as that which is given but revelation as that which is attained.

Even so, that which marks this document is the stress of the specifics of Jewish living. Hence we learn that

Our founders stressed that the Jew's ethical responsibilities, personal and social are enjoined by God. The past century has taught us that the claims made upon us may begin with our ethical obligations but they extend to other aspects of Jewish living . . creating a Jewish home . . . life-long study; private prayer and public worship , . . . keeping the Sabbath and the holy days . . . Reform Jews are called on to confront the claims of Jewish tradition.

It is interesting that there is no clear claim that ritual behaviors are divinely enjoined. Still, it is most instructive as to the changes occurring in Reform Judaism that the Reform Jew is instructed to confront the claims of Jewish Tradition.

Reform Judaism and Jewish tradition, Reform Judaism and *Halachah,* specificity without revelation, we have here a series of Reform Jewish oxymorons and yet a group of notions coherent with the American scene. For much of its history, America has been a country more interested in what worked than with ideology. This has been true for much of American Jewish life. Many Jews join congregations based on their liking the rabbi or their preferring the requirements (or the lack of them) for Bar/Bat Mitzvah or their being entranced by the building in which the particular congregation is housed. For such Jews, the specific identity and/or affiliation of the congregation is a secondary matter.

There has been another aspect of the American Jewish scene that up to very recently has been operative: it is ethnic identity. The majority of American Jews derive from Eastern Europe where Jewishness was perceived as an ethnic rather than a religious issue. One might be *frum* or not, pious or not, but one still affirmed Jewish identity.

It may well be that ethnic identity was that which in the past supported Zionism and that in the present supports Jewish ritual. It may also be that the American Jewish community is becoming more the same as most. American Jews have moved on the same socio-economic escalator to the middle-middle, upper middle, and upper classes. That being the case, we are not surprised to find Orthodox Jews sending their children to Ivy League colleges and Reform Jews sending their children on trips to Israel.

The sameness has made for a melding of symbols and rituals: *kippot* and *taletim* are found in Reform settings and *bat mitzvahs* and Women's Prayer groups are found in Orthodox settings. The Conservative Movement finds itself pulled in opposite directions: some Conservative Jews reject the ordination of women and other Conservative Jews are willing to accept gay people as rabbis.

We seem stuck between *ein keloheinu* with all its old meanings and its paraphrase "Who is like Thee, O Universal Lord?"! We wish to maintain Jewish tradition as if we believed in it in the same way that Jews in the past (to be precise, as some Jews in the past) believed it, but we wish to make innovations in the tradition when we find that some of it contravenes that which we have accepted from the liberal part of American culture. We may put on *tefillin*, but we will accept people whatever their sexual orientation. We will sing *aleinu l'shabei-ah,* but we will think "Let us adore the ever living God." We are Americans and Jews; we can choose—and we do choose!

But if we choose, we cannot say that we are bound by law – unless we say that we have chosen to be so bound; even so, the import of choice becomes the greater as we, as Liberal Jews, select among the vast array of Jewish behaviors, some to emulate and some to reject; to say that we are bound by what we choose is hardly to commit ourselves to the *Halakha*h as the past understood it.

Then why do we speak of Reform Jewish *Halakhah* – which to say the least is an oxymoron? I suspect it is for the same reason, that we sing *zot ha-Torah asher sam Mosheh* in the Torah service – certain terms and certain behaviors indicate our connection to what we perceive as the values of *k'lal yisrael,* the totality of the Jewish people. *Halakhah,* like *kippot,* are symbols of our intended togetherness with other Jews. Togetherness is indeed a value, but it is a partial value. For Liberal/Reform Jews, the necessity to make ethical changes and the pursuit of truth are higher values. We may use terms whose original meanings suggest notions that we don't share so long as we are clear in our minds what we mean by them.

God would still be the God of peace, if not external to the society, then certainly internally. Here then a kind of paradox: the notion that God was concerned with but one "religious" group in the society could not be maintained all the while the notion that God was concerned with the particular society was maintained. God would become "universal" all the while He was concerned with the fortunes of a particular nation state. The concept of a God interested in "everybody" would affect the concept of revelation.

Revelation, qua revelation, is, therefore, problematic for a secular society – and even for a society that has ostensible religious connections without starting up a *kulturkampf.* To live in society meant, at least in functional terms, that no one could or would make the claim that God had spoken to his particular group and has nothing to say to any member of the society. One may look to the reality of interfaith ministerial groups that embrace not only religionists of one or two persuasions, but religionists across the board. One can find any number of ministerial groups that include in their midst, ministers of the various Protestant faiths, Catholic priests, and rabbis. In fairness, one should note that this joining together is fairly new. On the other hand, the fact that in the military, chaplains of all persuasions are able to work together under the rubric of chaplains, forgetting for the moment their religious differences, is possible only in a society that is functionally secular, whatever its religious position. Only in such a society could chaplains of different positions agree to disregard their specific religious positions and work together. Every chaplain in the American military has to be able to deal with service persons who profess religions other than their own. No chaplain in the military is allowed to attempt to convert other service personnel to their own religious views. Indeed, to do so would be grounds for expelling that chaplain from the service.

For pragmatic purposes, different religions can do in a secular society that which they could not do in a religious society. One might argue that certain societies, e.g., Great Britain, ostensibly "religious" in terms of having established churches, are nonetheless secular in terms of civic operations.

Once the structural reality is understood, the problem of the shift in that reality and its effect on ideas and prescriptions for further behavior becomes most clear. To put the matter in the most extreme terms: no society could allow a religious group to execute a member of that group for heresy. No matter the religious provocation, the civil law overrides religious law, even if that law is taken to be the law of God. Whatever the sanctions once maintained by a particular religious group, those sanctions cannot be applied in the new situation without controverting civil law. It is civil law that controls the life of the citizens of the society and it must be so, since in the modern nation-state no one religion dominates and all religions are licit.

Religious groups within secular society may attempt to jockey for position, but such jockeying tends to be in matters of funding. Civil society to remain civil cannot allow one religion so to dominate others as to affect the nature of the society.

No matter how stated, there can be but one king in a secular kingdom and that is the head of state, however the state names him or her. So built into the system is a conflict between what may be said and what may be done, what may be believed, but not necessarily what can be believed in a nonfunctional way: the believer is free to believe that his/her own faith is the true faith and at the end of time all persons and indeed all members of the society will come to that conclusion: she/he is not free to impose that belief, however true she/he may feel it to be, on any other member of the society.

It must be said, however, that as religious groups entered the society, and we make Jews as a model of such entrance, the concept of God that supposedly structured the religion would be such as to be so general as to make specific life improbable, if not impossible.

Of course, the reader for whom Maimonides wrote would understand by "prophet" something quite different from that which the pious believe understood by the term.

Notes

1. Jacob Z. Lauterbach (ed.), *Mekhila de R. Ishmael, A Critical Ediction on the Basis of Manuscripts and Early Editions* with an English Translation, Introductions and Notes, Philadelphia, 1949, v. 2, *Masekhta Bahodesh, Parashah* 6, p. 239; henceforth quoated as Lauterbach.

2. Prov. 14:15.

3. Lauterbach, *Mechilta*, V. 3, *Masechechta deKaspa, Parashah* 4, p. 180.

4. In his comment on Ex. 20:2.

5. Samuel Rosenblatt (tr.), Saadia Gaon, *The Book of Beliefs and Opinions*, translated from the Arabic and Hebrew, New Haven, 1948, 7.1, p. 264; henceforth cited as Saadia.

6. Lauterbach, *Mechilta, Masekhta BaHodesh*, 5, pp. 229, 230.

7. Ex 19:6.

8. Hartwig Hirschfeld (tr.) Judah Halevi, *Kuzari*, New York, 1946, Part I, p. 32.

9. Saadia, 2:1, p. 118.

10. Saadia, 3:1; p. 139.

11. Halevi, 2:2, p.75.

12. Halevi, 2:2, p. 76

13. Halevi, 2:26, p. 89.

14. Halevi, 5:10, p. 228.

15. Shelomo Pines (tr.) Moses Maimonides, *Guide to the Perplexed*, Chicago, 1963, 3:45, p. 576. Henceforth cited as Maimonides.

16. Maimonides, 1:36, pp. 82 – 85

17. Maimonides 2:18, pp. 301, 302.

18. Maimonides 2:12, p. 279; 2:18, p. 300; 2:32, p. 361

19. Maimonides 2:32, p. 362.

20. Maimonides 2:35. p. 367.

21. Maimonides 2:36, p. 373

22. Ex 20:15.

23. Maimonides, 1:46. p. 100.

24. Maimonides, 2:46, p. 404.

25. Maimonides, 2:33, p. 364.

26. Maimonides, 28.

27. Maimonides, 29.

28. Maimonides, 11:2, p. 24.

29. Maimonides, 3:51, p. 620.

30. Maimonides, 3:27, p. 511.

31. Maimonides, 3:31, p. 524.

32. Heinrich Graetz, *History of the Jews*, Philadelphia, Vol. 5, p. 497.

33. Howard Sachar, *The Course of Modern Jewish History*, Cleveland, 1958, p. 63.

34. Is. 56:7.

35. Harry Austin Wolfson, *Crescas: A Critique of Aristotle: Problems of Aristotle's Physics in Jewish and Arabic Philosophy*, Cambridge, 1929.

36. For Crescas, the *Akedah* elicited *hesed*, God's steadfast love for the Jewish people. See E. Scheid (ed.), Hasdai Crescas: *Or Hashem*, Ferrara, 1555 (facsimile edition), Jerusalem 1970, 2:2, Chap. 6.

37. At the end of 2:2, Chap. 5, Crescas joins specific love to unique providence, as he observes that it would be highly improbable, and even impossible that one who knows and loves someone, would not provide providence for that one.

38. *Or Hashem*, 2:6, Chap. 2.

39. W. Gunther Plaut, *The Growth of Reform Judaism – American and European Sources until 1948*, New York, 1962, pp 96 – 100.

AUTONOMY, *HALAKHAH,* AND *MITZVAH:* ONLY IN AMERICA

Peter S. Knobel

The paper seeks to clarify four terms authority, autonomy, *mitzvah* and *halakhah*. The understanding of how these four concepts interact is necessary for understanding the way in which Reform Judaism makes decisions. The unique American context of Reform has affected the way in which these terms have come to function in the life of the Movement and in the lives of individual Reform Jews. Each reflects a perception of how decisions are made and what factors count in making such decisions. Since the Movement has no power to coerce and in American society a sense of collective authority has largely faded, the ultimate decisor is the individual. The deracinated individual sees him/herself as fully capable of determining his/her stand on most matters.

The challenge for Reform Judaism specifically and for Judaism in general is to make a compelling case as to why Jewish values and takes should significantly influence the decisions of individuals. Since in the United States Jewish identity and Jewish loyalty is a matter of choice, the Reform movement struggles to influence collective and individual decision making through the use of Jewish texts. The Freehof Institute of Progressive Halakhah and the Central Conference of American Rabbis (CCAR) Responsa Committee are the primary vehicles for sustained use of classical texts in the arriving at Reform Jewish positions on contemporary issues. In addition publications of the CCAR and the resolutions of the CCAR, Union for Reform Judaism (URJ), and the Religious Action Center (RAC) determine institution policy and place contemporary social and political issues into a Jewish context.

Walter Jacob in his article "The Law of the Lord is Perfect – *Halakhah* and Antinomianism," in *Reform Judaism* (*CCAR Journal* Summer 2004 pp. 72–84) writes, "There are some in our movement who have gone too far in their enthusiasm of halakhah and have rejected the rest of Reform Judaism. They have not understood that Reform Halakhah seeks to underpin and strengthen the major ideas of our movement, so important to all of Judaism, along with a good deal else. They have often seen the trees but not the forest of Judaism and so they have begun to ask questions about endless detail, perhaps, appropriate for Orthodoxy, but not us. We intend to recreate a *halakhah,* but not one that is either static or hidebound, and unchanging or tied principally to ritual. The strength of our movement has been a sense of balance, not always easily attained, but even as we strive for a better understanding of *halakhah* and incorporate *halakhah* into our Reform Jewish lives, we must remember its purpose is to strengthen and reinforce the major ideals of Judaism. Social justice, personal piety, the eternal Messianic dream of universalism must always be as central as the halakhic approach. Balance is never easy to achieve but it is always necessary."(pp. 81–82) The goal is, in effect, to create a non-binding *halakhah.*

In recent years there have been increasing attempts in the Progressive movement to utilize halakhic material to inform decision making in both the area of observance (*mitzvot bein adam lamakom*) and ethics (*mitzvot bein adam lehaveiro*). The reinvigoration of this enterprise is due in large measure to a changing ethos that has transformed Reform Judaism from a religion that relied largely on the Hebrew Bible, especially on a selective reading of the prophets, to a religion that seeks its authenticity more broadly in the whole of sacred literature. Our move from what might be characterized as a liberal

Protestant model – a kind of modern Karaism to a rabbinic model is the result of many factors, not the least of which are the Shoah, the rebirth of Israel, the rise of ethnicity with an attendant search for authenticity, and the demise of the Western philosophical models for creating authoritative positions.

A chronological examination of the Platforms of Reform Judaism from Pittsburgh 1885 to Pittsburgh 1999 provides a shorthand description of the development of contemporary American Reform Judaism. The Platforms begin with philosophical and theological certainty and move toward greater diversity and ambiguity. Reform Judaism moves from being confident that its break with many traditional rabbinic and biblical patterns represents Judaism as an authentic wave of the future that will supplant the others toward a broadly liberal group seeking relationship with and guidance from the totality of Jewish tradition. To comprehend this development it is necessary to cite the relevant passages from each platform in extenso.

Pittsburgh 1885

> We recognize in the Bible the record of the consecration of the Jewish people to its mission as the priest of the one God, and value it as the most potent instrument of religious and moral instruction. We hold that the modern discoveries of scientific researches in the domain of nature and history are not antagonistic to the doctrines of Judaism, the Bible reflecting the primitive ideas of its own age, and at times clothing its conception of

divine Providence and Justice dealing with men in miraculous narratives.

We recognize in the Mosaic legislation a system of training the Jewish people for its mission during its national life in Palestine, and today we accept as binding only its moral laws, and maintain only such ceremonies as elevate and sanctify our lives, but reject all such as are not adapted to the views and habits of modern civilization.

We hold that all such Mosaic and rabbinical laws as regulate diet, priestly purity, and dress originated in ages and under the influence of ideas entirely foreign to our present mental and spiritual state. They fail to impress the modern Jew with a spirit of priestly holiness; their observance in our days is apt rather to obstruct than to further modern spiritual elevation.

Columbus 1938

Torah. God reveals Himself not only in the majesty, beauty and orderliness of nature, but also in the vision and moral striving of the human spirit. Revelation is a continuous process, confined to no one group and to no one age. Yet the people of Israel, through its prophets and sages, achieved unique insight in the realm of religious truth. The Torah, both written and oral, enshrines Israel's ever-growing consciousness of God and of the moral law. It preserves the historical precedents, sanctions and norms of Jewish life, and seeks to mould it in the patterns of goodness and of holiness. Being products of historical processes, certain of its laws have lost their binding force with the passing of the conditions that called them forth. But as a depository of permanent spiritual ideals, the Torah remains the dynamic source of the life of Israel. Each age has the obligation to adapt the teachings of the Torah to its basic needs in consonance with the genius of Judaism.

San Francisco 1976

Reform Jews respond to change in various ways according to the Reform principle of the autonomy of the individual. However, Reform Judaism does more than tolerate diversity; it engenders it. In our uncertain historical situation we must expect to have far greater diversity than previous generations knew. How we shall live with diversity without stifling dissent and without paralyzing our ability to take positive action will test our character and our principles. We stand open to any position thoughtfully and conscientiously advocated in the spirit of Reform Jewish belief.

Within each area of Jewish observance Reform Jews are called upon to confront the claims of Jewish tradition, however differently perceived, and to exercise their individual autonomy, choosing and creating on the basis of commitment and knowledge.

Torah – Torah results from the relationship between God and the Jewish people. The records of our earliest confrontations are uniquely important to us. Lawgivers and prophets, historians and poets gave us a heritage whose study is a religious imperative and whose practice is our chief means to holiness. Rabbis and teachers, philosophers and mystics, gifted Jews in every age amplified the Torah tradition. For millennia, the creation of Torah has not ceased and Jewish creativity in our time is adding to the chain of tradition.

Pittsburgh 1999

We are committed to the ongoing study of the whole array of [*mitzvot*] and to the fulfillment of those that address us as individuals and as a community. Some of these (*mitzvot*), sacred obligations, have long been observed by Reform Jews; others, both ancient and modern, demand renewed attention as the result of the unique context of our own times.

Commentary to 1999. If "autonomy" was the key word of the Centenary Perspective, "dialogue" is the key word of the Pittsburgh Principles

Reflecting its time, the Centenary Perspective spoke of the need to secure the survival of the Jewish people, but confidently outlined what the Reform Movement had taught the Jewish world in its hundred years, and called on Reform Jews to confront the differently perceived claims of

Jewish tradition by "exercising their individual autonomy, choosing and creating on the basis of commitment and knowledge." It led to the phrase "informed choice" which along with "autonomy" became the watchwords of Reform Judaism.

As the platforms indicate there is an increasing interest in exploring Jewish practice and Jewish values using classic Jewish sources, especially rabbinic literature. This trend is exemplified in publication of two types of halakhic literature: a) codes of Jewish practice exemplified by *Gates of Mitzvah* and *Gates of the Seasons* and (b) those exemplified by responsa and by essays produced by the Freehof Institute for Progressive *Halakhah*.

Gates of Mitzvah and *Gates of the Seasons* may be understood as responses to the Centenary Perspective when there is a growing interest in traditional practice and the recovery of personal observance.

Our Religious Obligations: Religious Practice – Judaism emphasizes action rather than creed as the primary expression of a religious life, the means by which we strive to achieve universal justice and peace. Reform Judaism shares this emphasis on duty and obligation. Our founders stressed that the Jew's ethical responsibilities, personal and social, are enjoined by God. The past century has taught us that the claims made upon us may begin with our ethical obligations but they extend to many other aspects of Jewish living, including: creating a Jewish home centered on family devotion; lifelong study;

private prayer and public worship; daily
religious observance; keeping the Sabbath and
the holy days: celebrating the major events of
life; involvement with the synagogues and
community; and other activities which promote
the survival of the Jewish people and enhance
its existence. Within each area of Jewish
observance Reform Jews are called upon to
confront the claims of Jewish tradition, however
differently perceived, and to exercise their
individual autonomy, choosing and creating on
the basis of commitment and knowledge.

Gates of Mitzvah is a guide to daily living and to
critical moments in the Jewish life cycle. *Gates of the Seasons*
is a guide to the sacred calendar. Their goal is to set forth an
idealized and maximal Jewish practice. They are aimed at the
individual but they were also intended to influence the
movement as a whole. They by and large deal with religious
practice in the realm of *mitzvot bein adam lamakom*. They
offer simple statements that generally begin, "It is a **mitzvah** to
do or it is a *mitzvah* to refrain from doing." In each case there
is a justification as to why, and notes that seek to offer a source
from Jewish literature with the *Tanakh* being the preferred
source, followed in order by Mishna, Talmud, Maimonides and
then *Shulhan Arukh*. It is clear that they reflect a continuity
with the Reform preference for the *Tanakh* over rabbinic
literature. Whereas they use the word *mitzvah* to describe the
deed, the word remains untranslated and in *Gates of Mitzvah* is
the subject of four explanatory essays. *Mitzvah* has become, in
Reform, a term that mediates between commandment and good
deed. It is a value term that seeks to raise the level of deed
above that of mere personal choice, but is careful not to be
understood as mandatory. *Gates of Mitzvah* and *Gates of the*

Season are descriptive of important opportunities, not mandatory actions. They provide guidance and not governance. The fact that they utilize a quasir halakhic form is significant because it seeks to link Reform Judaism with Rabbinic Judaism and at the same time reflect the view of the Pittsburgh Platform, which maintain only such ceremonies as elevate and sanctify our lives.

The responsa, which in answering specific questions either addressed individual authority or more often to the Responsa committee, are more about a way of reasoning and decision-making that uses Jewish texts as a way of bringing guidance to an issue rather than an attempt to definitely decide the question. For us, halakhah is a way of thinking, not a set of decisions. Responsa seem increasingly to be about *mitzvot bein adam le haveiro,* specifically about the great ethical dilemmas we encounter in contemporary society and the boundary issues between Jews and non-Jews in an open society

Both forms of Reform's halakhic literature seek to reinforce that concept: We must never forget, though that was first and foremost how Jews related to 4000 years of Jewish history and related to 13 million Jews the world over. The burden of proof, therefore, must always be on those who want to abandon a particular tradition, not on those who want to retain it." (Rabbi Simeon Maslin, *Gates of the Seasons,* p. viii).

A single example from *Gates of the Seasons* should suffice to indicate the flavor of the character of *mitzvah* as portrayed in the guidebooks to practice.

In the section on Shabbat the second *mitzvah* listed is the *mitzvah* of joy (*oneg*). The description of this *mitzvah* is as follows:

It is a *mitzvah* to take the delight in Shabbat observance, as Isaiah said; You shall call Shabbat a delight (58:13). *Oneg* implies celebration and relaxation, sharing time with loved ones, enjoying the beauty of nature, eating a leisurely meal made special with conviviality and song, visiting with friends and relatives, taking a leisurely stroll, reading and listening to music. All of these are appropriate expressions of *oneg*. Because of the special emphasis on *oneg*, Jewish tradition recommended sexual relations between husband and wife on Shabbat.

A simple list of activities is not adequate to describe *oneg*, it is a total atmosphere is created by those activities that refresh the body and spirit and promote serenity (*Gates of the Seasons* p. 21).

The goal of this material is to make observance enticing. It is designed to be concrete enough to be clear but to be ambiguous enough for someone serious about to find his or her own definition of what activities are appropriate and what are inappropriate to fulfill this *mitzvah*.

The response literature provides rich examples of way in which the Reform movement seeks to provide guidance. CCAR Responsa 5763.6 Matriarch in the *Tefilah* illustrates both the reasoning of the committee and its own perceived lack of authority. The questioner accepts the concept that the Matriarchs should be included in the first blessing of the *Amidah* along with the Patriarchs raises questions about the way they are to be included, the order of Jacob's wives Leah and Rachel and finally whether Jacob's concubines should also be included. The responsum is a post hoc justification of current practice.

> The Matriarchs in the *tefilah*. [1] It has become the widespread *minhag* (custom) in our congregations to add the names of the *imahot*, the Matriarchs Sarah, Rebecca, Leah, and Rachel, to the names of the Patriarchs in the first benediction of the *tefilah*. [2] The motive for this change in the traditional prayer text was to express our understanding that *all* Jews, both male and female, participate equally in Israel's covenant with God and to give voice to the role of our Matriarchs in the transmission of that covenant to their descendants. This innovation is consistent with the liturgical tradition of the Reform movement, which from its inception has embraced the notion that the formal, public prayer recited in our synagogues should reflect our people's most deeply held values and commitments.

Then in what would be an unusual move in Responsa originating in the Orthodox and Conservative movement is a footnote that is as follows:

> It is not the function of this Committee to determine the text, structure, or wording of the new prayer book of the Central Conference of American Rabbis (CCAR). Those tasks belong to the prayer book's editors, as overseen by the CCAR Liturgy Committee. We therefore venture no opinion here as to the appropriate text of the new *siddur*. We consider this

she'elah rather because it touches upon a matter of Reform Jewish religious observance and, as such, does pertain to the function of this Committee.

The Committee makes it clear that even within the CCAR it does not have the authority to determine practice. Liturgical innovation in this case was a grassroots phenomenon and it was then sanctioned by the CCAR Liturgy Committee and the responsum provides additional explanatory material and a justification for liturgical innovation in the Reform movement.

A long and complex responsum "On the Treatment of the Terminally Ill" 5754.14, which deals with a myriad of issues including euthanasia and assisted suicide makes clear that there is a tension between historically accepted meaning of a text our Reform concept of finding new readings. The committee accepts the concept that since euthanasia is prohibited by the halakhah, even though some texts could be read as permitting it we should not do so. There must be a clear reason to deviate from the tradition. The responsum formulates it as follows: "As Reform Jews, of course, we consider ourselves free to ascribe 'new' Jewish meanings to Torah texts, to depart from tradition when we think it is necessary to secure an essential religious or moral value." This presents us with an example of the clash between autonomy and the authority of the tradition. If we give primary weight especially in making medical decisions to the patient, autonomy becomes the dominant value in decision making, this could then be supported by a new reading of the text. On the other hand if the value, the sanctity of life, and the concept that our bodies belong to God dominate our core values the committee believes the new reading is not legitimate. This has become part of the internal dialogue in Reform Judaism.

Before turning to the cases at hand in the responsum the committee provides a telling perspective about how responsa are to be understood.

> If this conviction leaves us in doubt as to the right answer for particular patients then it is well to remember that moral, religious, and halakhic truth can never be a matter of absolute certainty. There will always be more than one plausibly correct answer more than one possible application of our texts and our values to the case at hand Our task is to determine the best answer, one that most closely corresponds to our understanding of the tradition as a whole. That search must be conducted by means of analysis, interpretation, and argument. Its outcome will never enjoy the finality of the solution to a mathematical equation; its conclusions will be subject to challenge and critique. Yet this is no reason to shrink from moral arguments; it means rather that we have no choice but to enter the fray, to confront difficult cases, and to do the best we can. We may never be absolutely sure that we are right, but if we are thorough in our thinking, if we read the texts, consider the case, conduct our argument carefully and prayerfully, and that we can be sure that we have done our job.

In contemporary Progressive Judaism we have four concepts authority, autonomy, *mitzvah* and *halakhah*, which are interrelated. The interplay among them constitutes the inner dialogue of contemporary Judaism. The terms are never fully defined. In the current intellectual climate in the United States it is the dialogue between autonomy and authority and the desire for Jewish authenticity that place Reform Judaism in a unique position. Since we are open to the new and respectful of tradition, we have an opportunity to be creative and responsive. Our *halakhah* is nonbinding and pluralistic.

Authority in Reform Judaism is epistemic. The halakhic positions command obedience only in so far as they have the ability to convince the individual or the group that they are wise. Any Reform halakhic position so to speak is an authority but not in authority, because it has no power to coerce.

Autonomy as I understand the way the term is used in Reform Judaism refers to the concept that ultimately individuals are free to choose what they believe and do unencumbered by an external coercive authority.

Mitzvah is the name an individual or group apples to a deed that they believe commands special attention because it is sanctioned by tradition or is in response to a principle derived from tradition and confirms a core value of Reform Judaism. These deeds define individual and group core values and attempt to create or encourage specific practices that demonstrate a commitment to the core values.

Halakhah is the crystallization of an ongoing exercise in exegesis that seeks to provide a reasoned case based on traditional sources as to whether some practice is acceptable or not. This is especially true of the responsa literature produced by the CCAR Responsa committee, individual authorities like

Walter Jacob and Moshe Zemer and those who have written essays for the volumes produced by the Freehof Institute.

The progressive halakhic enterprise is a method of analysis designed to shape the behavior and ideas of those who engage in it. It is less about specific decisions than decision-making. It tries to persuade through an analysis of texts that seek to link contemporary decision making to historical tradition and thereby argue that it represents an authentic Jewish approach to contemporary dilemmas.

This confirms what Walter Jacob wrote and I cited at the beginning of the article.

> "We intend to recreate a *halakhah,* but not one that is either static or hidebound, and unchanging or tied principally to ritual. the strength of our movement has been a sense of balance, not always easily attained, but even as we strive for a better understanding of *halakhah* and incorporate, *halakhah* into our Reform Jewish lives, we must remember its purpose is to strengthen and reinforce the major ideals of Judaism. Social justice, personal piety, the eternal Messianic dream of universalism must always be as central as the halakhic approach. Balance is never easy to achieve but it is always necessary.

THE CASE OF FEMINISM – MECHANISMS OF CHANGE

Walter Jacob

Emancipation swept the old Jewish world away overnight. Nothing like that had happened for thousands of years. More radical changes were coming in the form of vast emigration, the Shoah, and the State of Israel. Judaism had to adapt quickly. The initial impulse, as always, was to do nothing and to reject any change in the words of Moses Sofer (1763–1839): "Any change is forbidden by the Torah."[1]

The old Jewish community, virtually "a state within a state" that governed itself was gone, and Jews, still without civil rights, were now treated as individuals in the new nation states. This revolution had been set in motion by Napoleon throughout his vast conquests. His new world view, with its promise of eventual civil rights and economic and social freedom, was hailed with joy by all Jews. Much of what he had promised and partially given was swept away with his defeat, but neither the ghetto walls nor the community of a "state within a state" could be reestablished by even the most conservative Central European states.

Jewish life had to be reconstituted and virtually reinvented as the community that had governed through Jewish law as a "state within a state"enforced by the Christian government was gone. The older mechanisms for change were no longer possible as communal authority was gone, the broader regional councils had disappeared and rabbinic decisions were ignored. Rabbis found their status, power, and decisions rejected. The Jewish individual with new-found freedom questioned everything. As Jews fought for equal rights and raised other issues in the new nation states, they also questioned every aspect of Jewish life that had thus far been taken for granted. This included the role of the *bet din*, synagogue services, the educational system, marriage and divorce laws, and everything else that was organized in such detail by the *Shulhan Arukh*. This soon included the place of women in Jewish life. Jewish women were in a better position than their gentile contemporaries as they could control property, trade, had a voice in their marriages, and could initiate divorce. These and other rights had been in place for centuries, but women were not equal to men, and especially in religious matters, their role was very limited and secondary. Voices demanding change were soon raised, but the change came haltingly in virtually every area; nor was a historical or theological basis for them developed. New mechanisms had to be invented and adopted to initiate change in this ans every sphere of Jewish life.

This paper will deal with the emerging mechanisms for change and innovation. I will show how these avenues evolved within the Reform Jewish community and eventually became valid for other segments of the newly fragmented Jewish society. Each community in this pluralistic Jewish world was a voluntary society, and anyone who was dissatisfied could join another group since persuasion had replaced coercion.

The successes and limitations of each of these mechanisms can best be shown by tracing a practical issue; I have chosen the slow awakening of feminism in the nineteenth and twentieth centuries. It illustrates these mechanisms well. The struggle for equal rights for women in Jewish life has been continuous until the present; this is in vivid contrast to most problems of the newly emancipated Jewish community, which were resolved long ago. Women have struggled[2] for two centuries. This paper will therefore deal with the creative methods used by the Reform community to deal with feminist issues. This should provide insight into the mechanisms of change used by the modern emancipated Jewish world as it shaped its future.

INDIVIDUAL INITIATIVE

The beginnings can be traced to Napoleon, both generally and specifically through the questions he addressed to the Assembly of 1806 and the Sanhedrin of 1807.[3] Napoleon's purpose was to integrate the Jewish community into the new French nation state. He had eliminated the power of the Catholic and Protestant churches as well as the guilds. He wished to move the Jews in that direction and used the technique of forcing the Jews, eager for civil rights, to address the issues themselves through a forum that would be widely recognized. He boldly chose the Sanhedrin, a halakhic mechanism, to which he addressed a series of questions.   The specific questions covered a broad range, but began oddly, with the question, "Are Jews allowed to marry several wives?" This was easily answered by citing the prohibition of a tenth century *takanah* attributed to Rabenu Gershom against polygamy.[4] The next two questions dealt with divorce and intermarriage and, of course, posed difficulties. The answers provided were straightforward, but skirted the *halakhah*, and did not deal with the feminist issues that might have been raised. The assembled delegates were not concerned with women's rights, nor for that matter was Napoleon.   No women were among the delegates, as was to be expected.

As the Jews of France wanted civil rights and needed to have Napoleon's ratification of those granted earlier by the Republic, they willingly gathered in an Assembly and later as a Sanhedrin without raising the issues of its authenticity or authority. Napoleon asked a few difficult questions but did not demand any changes in religious practices, so no objections were raised.[5] Protests could, of course, have been voiced against the very establishment of a Sanhedrin by a non-Jew, the composition of the Sanhedrin, the right of those assembled to respond to the questions, and so on, but this did not occur. The entire procedure could subsequently have been denounced quite safely outside the borders of lands conquered by the Emperor;

this also did not occur. In 1844, when a later assembly of rabbis began their discussions in Braunschweig with a re-examination of the responses of the Sanhedrin[6] that effort was also not denounced except by the Orthodox community. The broader Jewish community gladly accepted the new status Napoleon granted even if it did not mean complete civil rights and congratulated the Emperor. The Jewish community had been launched into a new world; the ends were used to justify the means.

The Sanhedrin Napoleon had so cleverly revived could have been the mechanism for all further changes that were needed. This would have been challenged by the emerging Orthodoxy, but as it objected to everything else, it would have been possible to modify the ancient institution and revive it as a halakhic mechanism However, no one even considered this step. The single reappearance of the Sanhedrin on the stage of modern Jewish history in 1806 was considered enough.

The initial steps for women's equality came from Israel Jacobson, the founder of the Reform movement, (1768–1828),[7] who established the first modern Jewish school for boys and girls in the small Jewish community of Seesen (Westphalia) in 1801.[8] Slightly later he introduced the ceremony of Confirmation, which represented graduation and coming of age for both boys and girls.[9] The establishment of this school for boys *and girls*, an innovation, was a personal decision of Jacobson and his coworkers, undertaken without halakhic discussion or rabbinic participation. The school in contrast to others of the same period followed a radical modern curriculum and was also open to non-Jewish students. A parallel step toward education specifically for girls also took place in 1801 in Dessau under the leadership of David Fraenkel (1779–1865), a well known *Maskil*, who enrolled twelve girls among his thirty students. The curriculum in that school was, however not innovative. Confirmation in Dessau was introduced for boys in 1809 and for girls in 1821.

Jacobson's move toward equality for boys and girls faced a mixed reaction, but brought no major halakhic opposition. The effort lapsed with the fall of the Kingdom of Westphalia in 1813; the new conservative regime did not permit further experiments in Jewish education or rituals. Jacobson was denounced for these efforts which he felt were necessary. He saw the need and proceeded; he continued to work in this direction in Berlin when it was no longer possible in Westphalia, but ran into governmental opposition there also.

The next step was taken by the Hamburg Temple (dedicated in 1818) in the more liberal climate of that city. Its service included prayers in German partly to appeal to women, who knew little Hebrew and wished to participate in the service. There also was a sermon in German. Forty-three percent of the seats were designated for women, a much higher percentage than in Orthodox synagogues.[10] The contemporary scholar, Aaron Chorin (1766 – 1854) was among those who felt that Jewish services should appeal to both sexes.[11] The Hamburg Temple effort, of course, depended upon the good-will of the government which retained the power to supervise Jewish religious life. As most of the states of Central Europe in the post-Napoleonic period feared innovations, no matter how minor, we see how exceptional Hamburg was. The other states and cities saw any change as a forerunner of revolution. At the same time, the work of the educator Pestalozzi brought large scale educational reforms throughout Europe and influenced the general and Jewish patterns of education. Jewish education was fragmented, disorganized, and often left to poorly trained teachers.[12]

In Hamburg change was accomplished by the leadership of one synagogue without any broad-scale discussions. In Seesen, Breslau, Dessau, Frankfurt, and other cities which experimented with new educational efforts, a single individual brought about decisive changes. In the new free setting an individual or a single institution could experiment or bring changes at least on a local scale. It was now possible to work outside the framework of the *Halakhah*. This freedom had not existed in the Jewish communities of the Middle Ages. We shall see it used again later and then better understand its positive implications and its limitations.

THE HISTORICAL APPROACH

Abraham Geiger (1810–1874), the intellectual father of Reform Judaism, surveyed the Jewish past broadly through historical studies[13]. He demonstrated that Judaism had developed and adapted constantly through the ages. Therefore there was no reason to hesitate to undertake changes now desirable. Such an approach made it possible for him to make an early appeal for the proper education of women; this was part of a report on youth education in Bavaria, Prussia, Westphalia, and the smaller states which he published in his journal;[14] we do not know of any positive response. These educational steps were neither defended on halakhic grounds by the incipient Reform movement nor attacked by the Orthodox initially. Perhaps they felt that the conservative states would not permit them anyhow. They were right since all initiatives got under way slowly. By the later half of the nineteenth century, however, the Orthodox communities, especially those influenced by Samson Raphael Hirsch, founder of modern Orthodoxy, (1808–1888), followed a parallel path for young women's education.[15]

Prayers in the vernacular could and were easily defended through rabbinic statements; we should note, however, that such translations were not undertaken primarily for the benefit of women. When Mendelsohn's translations of the Bible into high German appeared, it was attacked mainly out of fear of what would come next. This was the basis for the opposition in 1791 of Ezekiel Landau, Moses Sofer and their disciples to Moses Mendelssohn's Torah translation. Landau realized that traditional Judaism could not reject this effort on the basis of the tradition but saw it as a dangerous opening to the outside world.[16] Another Orthodox leader, Jacob Emden regretted that his father had not given him a general education, but opposed the new systematic general studies as they neglected the traditional material.[17]

Abraham Geiger was the first to connect innovation to the *halakhah* through his historical studies, which demonstrated that Judaism had evolved and that changes had always taken place.[18] Geiger showed that the changes in the liturgy as well as those that he suggested for marriage and divorce were part of a continuum. He demonstrated that Jewish women, despite all short-comings, were treated better in the biblical period than were women in the surrounding culture[19] and that their condition improved gradually later. The Talmud and subsequent rabbinic literature continued in this direction, albeit with centuries in which progress was scant. Geiger therefore felt that basic changes in such difficult areas as *agunah, halitzah*, and divorce were legitimate by pointing to major changes that had taken place in the past, prompted by new conditions in the surrounding society.[20]

Geiger's innovation lay in the justification for change through his developmental approach to Jewish history. Halakhic precedent by itself may have been insufficient, but viewed historically, Judaism could be seen in a developmental framework, not as eternally stable. The continuous development was influenced by the surrounding world as well as the internal conditions of Jewish life.   This was also Zacharias Frankel's (1801–1875) view although he limited it to the rabbinic period. Here was a pattern that provided an ideological basis for many different type of change, including changes in the status of women.

Geiger followed the path on which his studies had led him into the practical realities of the times. While rabbi of Wiesbaden (1837) at the age of twenty-seven he called on his colleagues to make the following changes in the status of women:

> 1. A declaration of death by the state would be sufficient to free an *agunah*.
> 2. As soon as the state issued a divorce document, it was to be considered valid even though the husband might refuse to provide the traditional *get* or express willingness to do so only through extortive conditions.
> 3. *Halitzah* should be removed, abrogated entirely, and in any case, be deemed unnecessary if the obligated brother could not be found or if his wife objected.

Geiger justified this new approach through his developmental view of the Tradition, though he understood very well that a different interpretation of the Tradition would not permit any of these changes.[21] Here we have a broad and sweeping approach as Geiger pointed to radical transformation of the past as his guideposts; they had often been made without detailed justification or any real roots in the more distant past. They would, nevertheless, eventually be anchored in the past and provided with some ties to the *halakhah*.

Geiger provided a theoretical basis for the changes that his generation considered necessary and made it clear that they were fully justified. His view of history destroyed the notion of an eternally stable Judaism that allowed for no adaptation or innovation. As Judaism had evolved throughout its history, there was no reason to hesitate now. This was a bold theory and provided an intellectual foundation for the reconstruction of Judaism that was necessary to face the newly emancipated world.

RESPONSA AND THER INNOVATIONS

The need for discussion and agreement on a practical path was clear. Individual adjustments in matters of marriage, divorce, synagogue liturgy, and a good deal else no longer sufficed. Changes had been made in many communities by rabbis in accordance with their personal theological position and based on what was possible in a particular community.

Some efforts at a unified position had been made through the classical pattern of responsa which provided decisions and justified innovations. Individual responsa as well as published collections brought the opinions of colleagues. They were especially useful in the defense of liturgical innovations. These responsa marked the beginning of an effort to work together. They focused on major changes in the liturgy and on a most audible innovation, the use of the organ – which became a symbol of liturgical reform.[22] The Reform responsa immediately led to an Orthodox response, and these exchanges continue for a few years. Then they diminished and were briefly restimulated when the radical Reform Society of Frankfurt toyed with the notion of eliminating the _b'rit milah_ – something rejected by Orthodox and Reform Jews alike.[23]

This halakhic path, brief as it was in Reform circles, contained the innovation of responsa in the German vernacular that appeared alongside Hebrew responsa. This step sought a broader readership and no longer limited the discussion to rabbis. This innovation interestingly paralleled the move of the _haskalah_, then and earlier, in the opposite direction in its effort to revive literary exchanges in Hebrew, something that remained most effective in eastern Europe. We should note that all these responsa dealt with liturgical matters and none with feminist issues. Responsa in the vernacular did not reappear until the very end of the nineteenth century and then in America, not Europe.[24]

These responsa never dealt with feminist issues in the liturgy, even when they should have. So the omission in some early Reform prayer books of the statement, "You have not made me a woman" was not turned into an issue. It is true that Abraham Geiger objected vigorously to the traditional explanation that it merely indicated that the male thanked God for the obligations of assuming the commandments.[25] This specific change , however, did not lead to any thorough discussion, perhaps because it was one of many changes in the liturgy that were far more radical, such as dropping the *musaf* service, eliminating the repetition of the *amidah,* and rejecting virtually all *piyutim.* Jakob Petuchowsky's masterful study of the liturgical innovations and the reaction they brought, does not mention any discussion of this *berakhah.*[26] David Novak, who subsequently analyzed this *berakhah* and its meaning, indicated that there was little interest in this change among the traditionalists when it was made by the early Reform movement.[27] The expansion of the women's section in various synagogues and the elimination of barriers which had hidden women also was rarely discussed.

Responsa in the hands of a single decisive charismatic scholar could have provided a path toward change but the voices of democracy were too strong and the broad nature of the issues too overwhelming. Furthermore responsa were a rabbinic tool and did not appeal to the broader community even when written in German; they sought changes and were satisfied with less detailed explanations for them. Much of the Reform rabbinate was also more interested in rebuilding Judaism for the contemporary world than in the slow process of justifying innovations and discussing them in detail. Therefore the rabbinate chose a different path.

THE DEMOCRATIC APPROACH

Abraham Geiger was not only a theoretician, but a very practical leader. He proposed a a gathering of rabbis to deal with the problems of the community and the issues that faced his colleagues. The rabbinic colleagues as well as Geiger felt a need for collegiality in facing the numerous changes being made which needed common solutions as well as a united defense. Geiger had considered this problem as early as 1837 and expressed it in private correspondence; he made it public through repeated calls for a rabbinic meeting in *Jeschurun.* Such a meeting of rabbinic colleagues took place in Wiesbaden in August 1837 and was attended by 16 rabbis, but the only practical result was consensus that a larger meeting should be held soon. Continuous pushing on the part of Geiger and the efforts of Ludwig Philippson (1811–1889), the editor of the *Allgemeine Zeitung.* Along with other factors led to the first major rabbinic meeting in 1844 in Braunschweig.[28]

Although halakhah would play a role, a new and different path was to be taken by three rabbinic meetings that took place in rapid succession in Braunschweig (1844) that was attended by twenty-five rabbis; followed a meeting in Frankfurt (1845) attended by thirty, and one in Breslau (1846), with twenty-four rabbi present.[29] The numbers remained relatively small as many states and principalities did not permit their rabbis to attend. Those that came represented a wide range of views from conservative to liberal, but Orthodox rabbis stayed away and awaited the direction which these meetings would take,[30] as the meetings and their purpose was an innovation. This group of rabbis had, after all, gathered to make decisions.

Rabbis gathering to make decisions had a long history with many medieval precedents.[31] Yet there was a major difference in these meetings as most of the earlier conferences dealt with taxation, fiscal policy, and economic regulations. They were often initiated or approved by the Christian government that then supported their decisions, as they led to a more efficient way of collecting taxes. Anyhow the government did not want to get involved in the details of the Jewish communities. Their status of a "state within a state" permitted this approach. There councils also dealt with issues of family law and ritual matters. When such questions however, arose, they turned to the halakhic authorities for direction which was sometimes innovative, but always deeply rooted in the *halakhah*. Innovations did occur, but no radical changes. The three nineteenth century rabbinic conferences were to deal with status, the structure of family life and the liturgy of the synagogue in a totally open and democratic way. Anything could be questioned and was open to debate.

The rabbis adopted the democratic process that they saw around them. There were references to the limited democracy that had existed in the medieval councils but they were not interested in earlier precedents. This open democratic approach represented an enormous innovation and was to be the major path of all Jewish communities in the future. This path was adopted without discussion or protest as it fitted the times and the mood of those who attended. Furthermore, the deliberations, not only the conclusions would be publicized. The rabbis realized that in this new emancipated world their authority was limited to their persuasive powers. Innovations and changes had to be voluntarily accepted and could not be imposed since the Jewish communities no longer possessed any enforcing power.

Those assembled at Braunschweig saw themselves continuing the work of Napoleon's Sanhedrin, which had been organized democratically. It had legitimized changes sought by the French emperor, but the rabbis at Braunschweig did not consider their assembly a Sanhedrin. They knew that the ancient Sanhedrin had been an institution capable of innovation and change, but tradition had surrounded it with enough restrictions to read it out of existence. It remained as a purely theoretical device. It existed on paper, but in practice could not be reconstituted.[32] They decided to function as a democratic assembly, a major innovation in itself.

A second innovation followed, as the proceedings were carried out in the vernacular and then published in the vernacular as well. Thus the proceedings were open and transparent; the attendees, of course, recognized that fluency in Hebrew among their congregants had become limited. This step also represented an effort to influence the broader community as widely as possible, which was clearly stated in the introduction of the published proceedings.

The Brauschweig Conference and its successors were democratic institutions with votes determining decisions; halakhic debate had its influence but was not the determining factor. Rabbinic authorities had no veto powers. In other words the democratic institution of the outside world had been adopted to guide the path toward change within Judaism. This set a pattern for the entire Jewish world; even within the Orthodox community democracy within limits would reign in the future.

Abraham Geiger and those who presided understood the limitations of democratic procedures. The proceedings could easily grind to a halt and block any decision. They therefore frequently used the tools that had been worked out in the broader society – referral to committee, postponement, and parliamentary procedures. Geiger and others also realized that halahkic and philosophical discussions among rabbis who needed to express their personal opinions would be divisive and would hinder conclusions on the practical issues that faced the conference, so they agreed from the outset to avoid or curtail such discussions.[33]

The innovation, therefore, lay in the conference itself and the manner in which it was conducted. Views at both ends of the spectrum – radical and conservative – would influence the practical decisions, but would be kept within bounds. This meant that individuals such as the more conservative Zacharias Frankel, generally considered the father of Conservative Judaism, (1801–1875) could not destroy a meeting, but would simply leave and express their views outside its meetings.[34] The new system worked, although these rabbis represented divergent backgrounds and came with different education, some from *yeshivot* while others were university trained. This would influence their outlook on such specific issues as matters of status (marriage, divorce, *halitzah*) and liturgical innovations where confusion reigned and some agreement was necessary, though some were disappointed that a more theoretical approach was not taken.[35] Although the meeting was open to Orthodox rabbis, none attended as they understood the liberal agenda the organizers would press. Although women's issues arose often and were decided in a positive way, the underlying status of women was not discussed.

These meetings also provided a symbol of unity to the Jewish community – not a perfect by far, but at least a start. The Braunschweig Conference began its discussions with a review of the work of the Napoleonic Sanhedrin of 1807. The Conference looked at some of the implications but mainly from a practical point of view. There was no discussion of the underlying premises: no one asked about the validity of a Sanhedrin or Assembly called by a non-Jewish ruler to radically change the Jewish community. As the rabbis that gathered in Braunschweig did not have Napoleon looking over their shoulders and were dealing with a *fait accompli*, they faced the issues it raised but also continued one element of the Sanhedrin by emphasizing their patriotism. When they reviewed the response of the Sanhedrin on intermarriage, they let it stand with a proviso that the children be raised as Jews when permitted by the government, a permission granted by none in the 1840s. Nor was it yet an issue in their communities. The halakhic issues that the Sanhedrin had avoided were not raised nor were philosophical questions We should note that the Sanhedrin was never discussed in the later Reform rabbinic meetings in Europe or North America.

THE PLACE OF TRADITION

These new open democratic procedures were welcome and accepted. They soon led to a major question: should decisions be based only on contemporary considerations even when it meant a major break with the past, or should the Tradition and *halakhah* play a dominant role. The two ends of the spectrum were represented in these conferences by Samuel Holdheim (1806–1860) and Samuel Adler (1809–1891) who became rabbi at Temple Emanu-El, New York in 1857). Adler's position was close to Geiger's view of the historical development of Judaism, but Adler also felt that innovations should be anchored in the halakhic tradition.[36] A major debate on this issue at the meeting was avoided, although it could have occurred a number of times. It threatened to break out over feminism and the status of women in Judaism. The confrontation did not occur; the views of Samuel Adler, however, were published as an appendix in the volume of proceedings of the conference. There, Adler presented a lengthy Hebrew essay defending the changes in the status and role of women by citing halakhic precedents, although often interpreted differently from the Tradition. Holdheim initially responded briefly but then in a lengthy German pamphlet. Both these reform leaders favored complete equality for women and were thinking far beyond the liturgical changes and those in the matrimonial law contemplated at the sessions, but they disagreed on the theoretical basis for such changes.[37]

In this exchange we can see a different approach to the halakhic material, not through an authoritative and binding responsum, but through persuasive essays. The old power of imposing an answer and enforcing it had disappeared. Now those that deliberated innovation had to be persuaded that the *halakhah* had bearing on the matter under discussion and that it should be heard and accepted. The new approach included looking at the halakhic material within the historical and sociological conditions of its time, raising divergent views rejected long ago, or totally reinterpreting the *halakhah*. Each of these paths was suggested by Adler and was made part of his proposal for a basic review of the position of women as one can see through a quick review of his essay, reprinted as an appendix to this volume.

The essay of Samuel Adler is thoroughly argued; it knowingly took liberties with the *halakhah.* which has always been a way of expanding the *halakhah.* At the subsequent meeting in Breslau (1846) a similar paper in German was given by J. Auerbach (1810–1887); it provided many parallel citations.[38] This time a discussion of biblical and talmudic texts could not be avoided. Adler then proposed a far reaching resolution on feminism. He read a six point program was read to the Conference; it was the most thorough statement on the rights of women to be suggested at these meeting:

> We recommend that the rabbinical conference declare woman to be entitled to the same religious rights and subject to the same religious duties as man and in accordance herewith make the following pronouncements:
>
> 1. That woman are obliged to perform such religious acts as depend on a fixed time, in-as-far as such acts have significance for our religious consciousness.
> 2. That women must perform all duties toward children in the same measure as man.
> 3. That neither the husband nor the father has the right to release from her vow a daughter or a wife who has reached her religious majority.
> 4. That the benediction *shelo asani ishah* (Praised be You, O Lord, our God who has not made me a woman), which owed its origin to the belief in the religious inferiority of women be abolished.
> 5. That the female sex is obligated from youth up to participate in religious instruction and the public religious

service and be counted for *minyan*; and finally,

6. That the religious majority of both sexes begin with the thirteenth year.[39]

This resolution which went further than anything previously suggested was discussed briefly but then tabled for action at the next rabbinic meeting which did not materialize. Many of the same matters, however, – marriage, divorce, *halitzah*, Shabbat,, holidays, and liturgy generally – were brought up again at the synod held in Leipzig in 1869. This meeting and the following synod included lay leaders along with rabbis. The second synod, which followed in Augsburg, continued to deal with some of these practical issues, but neither undertook a broad look at the status of women. The rabbis attending the Braunschweig Conference may have been prepared for a summary of the changes that they had already made but not for the concluding point five which went further but they but also did not want to vote negatively, so it was tabled.

The disagreement between Adler and Holdheim was fundamental to the direction of the Reform movement. Holdheim, who was a talmudic scholar, was willing to review the rabbinic tradition but equally willing to make radical changes when necessary outside that tradition. He had stated his position quite clearly at the beginning of the conference and sought numerous occasions to turn the debates to a broader discussion of principle.[40] He felt sufficiently strongly about Adler's essay to write a sixty-page pamphlet that discussed Adler's monograph point by point; it was published separately in Schwerin in 1846.

This debate on the basis for change ran parallel to the rabbinic conferences, but was not part of them, so that its divisive force would not delay or possibly destroy the meetings. This very fact demonstrated that a new way of proceeding had quickly and quietly been adopted. There was enough feeling for the older path of anchoring everything in the *halakhah* so that Adler's lengthy essay was published as an appendix. This may also reflect an attempt to include the more traditional rabbis that had not attended the conferences either because of governmental prohibitions or their own hesitation.

This effort to establish a theoretical basis for decisions either before making decisions through a majority vote or alongside it would certainly have been possible, but it was not followed on this occasion and generally discarded both in the Old World and the New World.

The Philadelphia Conference of 1869 followed the pattern of the three earlier German rabbinic meetings. The meeting was organized by David Einhorn (1809–1879) and Samuel Adler, who had also recently immigrated to North America; it was held in June – the same time as the synod in Leipzig. All the participants were Reform rabbis, many of whom had been part of the earlier conferences and were still most at home in the German language which was used for the meetings.[41]   The sessions paralleled those of the European meetings, however, they brought more theological discussions and frequent references to the *halakhah* on marriage, divorce, *aguna, halitzah* and *yibbum.*   Although halakhic concerns were mentioned, there were few long citations and no major statement such as Adler's earlier paper. The Atlantic Ocean created a great divide. No one felt any urgency to mount a major defense of innovations since all the rabbis served Reform congregations, not mixed communities as in Germany. The purpose of the meeting was also similar, that is to bring the rabbis of the New World together and to establish a pattern of Jewish life which would be more uniform – something even more necessary in America than in Europe as the new Jewish settlers were still seeking a pattern for their congregations.

The proceedings of the meeting were summarized and the total material was published in German and was therefore generally available. It meant that many practical issues were now settled for those already in America and for the constant stream of newcomers. Despite the theological discussions, no broad statements were adopted; nor was a clear position on the status of women.

The Central Conference of American Rabbis organized by Isaac Mayer Wise in 1889, followed democratic procedures and was determined to meet annually to present a forum for discussion of major and minor. Its structure provides continuity which escaped the earlier rabbinic meetings. Its deliberations, resolutions, and responsa continue to provide a path toward change within the Reform Jewish community alongside its lay counterpart the Union of Reform Judaism. The democratic process of resolutions was and continues to be used to deal with many issues. It involved the Conference heavily in contemporary issues of all kinds, and brought Jewish views to the attention of the broader public.

The process of resolutions was quickly refined by the Conference, Resolutions were initially brought to a committee by individuals or groups of rabbis. They were then debated with the committee, rejected or refined at this level, and then sent to the broader conference for further discussion. This process avoided unwieldy discussion at the annual meetings. This mechanism has proven useful for more than a century. The resolutions were placed into the framework of the Jewish tradition in a general way and usually without a thorough review of the past. That was left to the Reponsa Committee if it wished to undertake the task or to individual rabbis.

In 1893 the Central Conference adopted a resolution on the status of Jewish women:

WHEREAS, We have progressed beyond the idea of the secondary position of women in Jewish congregations, we recognize the importance of their hearty cooperation and active participation in congregational affairs; therefore be it RESOLVED that the Executive Committee have prepared a paper tracing the development of the recognition of women in Jewish congregations, and expounding a conclusion that women be eligible for full membership, with all privileges of voting, and holding office in our congregations.[42]

Any citing of traditional material would await a full paper. The paper which was to follow in the subsequent year, however, did not materialize. This resolution went further than any earlier statement. It came in the same year as the World Parliament of Religions met in Chicago with two papers on women in Judaism. Dr. Landsberg dealt largely with the biblical period, but noted the changes of the nineteenth century. Ms. Szold provided a review of the past, but concentrated on the modern period, however, with little about the problems remaining.[43] The Congress of Jewish Women also participated in that meeting.[44]

The American women's movement faced a long, tough, uphill battle for the right to vote which finally occurred through the ratification of the nineteenth amendment in 1920. This was the next step for women's rights which needed support. A number of prominent rabbis were heavily involved. However the Central Conference was slow to take a stand, yet the resolution process eventually worked. We will trace it through the years to demonstrate this democratic path. An effort in 1913 to place a resolution before the Conference failed. The proposed resolution in part reads:

That this Central Conference of American Rabbis by common recognition the largest and most representative organization of progressive Judaism today in the entire world, places itself on record as a body in sympathy with and in support of the latest appeal for the extension of liberty in civilization and recommends that its members individually in their pulpits and through their ministries, advocate and advance the cause of women's equal political suffrage with man's.

The committee on resolutions, however, rejected this proposed resolution by stating "that this is a matter for the individual rabbi and deems it inadvisable for the Conference as a body to take action."[45] The issue was revisited in 1915 with the proposal of a similar resolution, but with eleven signatures and the statement

> Whereas, the question of Women's Suffrage will be presented to the voters of a number of States in the course of the year, Be it resolved that the Conference places itself on record as favoring the enfranchisement of women.

It was once more rejected on the basis that this was a matter for the individual rabbi.[46] A stronger resolution was proposed in 1917 that cited our own suffering through discrimination as well as the patriotism of women and concluded that

> We, the Central Conference of American Rabbis, hereby feel it to be our solemn duty, as preachers of a religion which has stood throughout the centuries for justice and righteousness, to assert our belief in the justice and righteousness of the enfranchisement of the women of our country.

This was signed by 18 rabbis. The vote of the committee was divided with the majority in favor and a minority opposed. The resolution was then adopted.[47]

Further statements on numerous issues which faced women continued to come from the Central Conference and the Union for

Reform Judaism. Other organizations grew out of the Reform movement as new needs became apparent. First among them was the National Federal of Temple Sisterhoods, now Women for Reform Judaism, founded in 1918. In 1972 following the ordination of a number of women as rabbis, the Women's Rabbinic Network was founded. Each of these organizations of the Reform movement, along with others, have dealt with a broad range of women's issues. Their concerns went beyond the immediate Jewish matters and ranged from the White Slave Trade to Reproductive Rights.[48] The Social Action Center of Reform Judaism has played a major role since 1959 and often spoken for the entire Jewish community on major causes including women's issues.[49]

As women rabbis began to play an increasing role in the affairs of the Conference, women headed committees and served as its president.[50] A gender neutral prayer book, which appeared in 2004, was the natural further step in this direction.

In the New World even more than in the Old, the democratic pattern became a major path of settling issues. The rabbis who were familiar with the path of responsa but chose not to take it. The pattern for creating changes in this manner, first introduced in Europe, found an even greater welcome in North America.

Each of these steps proceeded through the democratic process which had become the central agent of change. In contrast to earlier times, democracy prevailed in all matters without any   limitations.

THE *MINHAG*

America used a time honored path for innovation – the *minhag* (the voice of the people) often. This was relatively easy as there were no restrictions and complete religious freedom. Isaac Mayer Wise (1819–1900), the founder of the democratic Reform organizations, was also willing to follow the path of the *minhag*. He understood the need for organizations and had been present at the rabbinic meeting in Frankfurt, but he also understood that they move slowly. He was a proponent of equality for women and instituted the family pew which immediately became popular. The people saw it as a new *minhag*. The family pew, introduced by Isaac Mayer Wise in his Albany congregation was denounced by Isaac Leeser (1806–1868) in *The Occident* in1851,[51] but it rapidly became widely accepted. There was neither national outcry nor national debate. The seating of women with men was gradually adopted. It became the norm in Reform and many Conservative congregations without halakhic justification as did counting women as part of a *minyan* which fits well already into Isaac Mayer Wise's early thoughts.[52]   Here was a major step forward toward the equality of women, taken quietly. It was followed by changes in marriage and funeral ceremonies and women on synagogue boards, along with other matters.

Isaac Mayer Wise and other Reform leaders never became leaders for change in the broader feminine issues. They remained uninfluenced by the events around them as for example, the first North American effort in this long struggle occurred in Seneca Falls, N. Y. In 1848. Of all the great revolutionary events of that year, this was the quietest. On July 19–20, 1848, a two day "convention" took place in a small Wesleyan chapel whose minister became reluctant when the meeting date approached. It was barely noted in the local paper. There were a large number of subsequent meetings in the next decade, often denounced, especially by religious leaders; women were divided over whether to demand the vote or not. When the 14th amendment, which gave rights to the Negro was proposed in 1866, a few raised the issue of women's rights, whereas some still wondered whether women were considered citizens.[53] The Supreme Court unanimously decided that citizenship did not confer the right to vote in 1874. The American women's movement was slow in getting started and faced a long, tough, uphill battle, until the equal rights amendment of 1920.

Individual Jewish leaders spoke out, but the organized community in North America did not although some Jewish women were suffragettes. A conservative wait and see attitude prevailed as it did in much of American society through those decades. The path of the *minhag* would bring only limited changes.

In the democratic setting of North America, the voice of the people could force innovation. This was an extension of the *minhag* which has been a major force in Jewish life throughout our history; the rabbinate resisted, reluctantly accommodated, or ignored these *minhagim*, especially if they were contrary to the halakhic tradition.[54] In numerous instances such divergent paths were, nevertheless taken. For example the Talmud ignored semi-pagan synagogue decorations which continued for centuries in Israel and the neighboring lands. Rabbis frequently accepted a local *minhag* in liturgy and in life-cycle ceremonies, such as breaking the glass at weddings or permitting pictures on tombstones. It was more difficult to resist in America even when the change was as drastic as mixed seating. Innovations occurred and spread without any attempt at halakhic justification. This was true of scores of innovations great and small and certainly of every move in the direction of feminism such as women's Torah reading, *bat mitzvah*, women in leadership positions and eventually the admission of women to rabbinic studies. All these changes occurred as *minhag*. In America *minhag* reigns supreme. The *minhag* has been a dominant force on the American Jewish scene, affecting every aspect of Jewish life. It, of course, represents popular democracy.

A THEOLOGICAL APPROACH

Kaufmann Kohler (1843 – 1926), who came to the United Sates from Germany in 1869 felt the need for a broader statement of modern Judaism that would go beyond practical changes. He had not instigated anything like this in Germany, perhaps as he saw it too difficult in those communal settings and with the conservative governments. He did what Samuel Holdheim might have undertaken. However, he did not limit himself to writing, but used a meeting. Kohler understood the divide between the radical Reform rabbis in the East and the more conservative western rabbis led by Isaac Mayer Wise in Cincinnati. In 1885 Kohler therefore called a meeting in Pittsburgh, neutral territory half way between the two camps. It provided an opportunity to create a document that would go beyond the specific decisions of Philadelphia and place them into an ideological setting. Kaufmann Kohler came with a fully prepared text that with some modifications became the Pittsburgh Platform.

This represented another major innovation. Creedal statements had been created by some leading thinkers of the past, including Maimonides (1135–1204). Even this statement of the greatest medieval Jewish scholar was never fully accepted by the Jewish community, although it is printed in the private devotions of the traditional prayer book. Here, however, was a statement of principles that was adopted by a group of rabbis for a the Reform movement. It dealt with theology, the entire range of religious life and observance[55] and represented a striking innovation. As the Reform movement changed similar documents were later prepared, debated, and became the official pronouncement of the Central Conference of American Rabbis and of the Reform movement. This occurred in Columbus (1937), San Francisco (1976), and Pittsburgh (1999).

Kohler was concerned about the position of women in Reform Judaism and in modern Jewish life. The address presented to the assembled rabbis, therefore, included a major section on women and pointed to all that women do for religious life and education.

> They do the work of charity everywhere, and their sympathies are broader and more tender than those of the stern struggler for existence in the business mart. Indeed, none of the greater

time-absorbing tasks of Congregational life is discharged with the same self-denying devotion and enthusiastic zeal by our men, few of whom find even the time for our Sabbath School work on Sunday, as it would be done by ladies. Our religious life in America demands woman's help and participation. And I do not hesitate to claim for myself the priority of the claim for *women's* full admission *into the membership* of the Jewish Congregation. Reform Judaism has pulled down the screen from the gallery behind which alone the Jewish women of old was allowed to take part in divine service. Reform Judaism has denounced as an abuse the old Hebrew benediction: "Blessed be God who has not *made me a woman*," borrowed from Plato who, notwithstanding his soul's lofty flights in the highest realm of thought, never realized the high dignity of women as the co-partner and helpmate of man. Reform Judaism will never reach its higher goal without having first accorded to the congregational council and in the entire religious and moral sphere of life, equal voice to woman with man.[56]

No statement of this nature, however, found its way into the Pittsburgh Platform and we do not know why. The broad outline of the published proceedings contains no discussion of any portions of this major document. This may have been intentional in order to provide a show of ideological unity. The Platform was radical and including a paragraph on women should have caused no concern. The bold statements which set the course for what was called "Prophetic Judaism" was not extended to women at this meeting. .

The radical Pittsburgh Platform adopted in 1885 followed the democratic pattern set forty years earlier. It made a conscious break with the past and contained no halakhic references whatsoever.[57] Oddly enough, discussions on specific ritual matters toward the latter part of the meeting cited traditional texts.

Earlier Isaac Mayer Wise's *American Israelite* or Isaac Leeser's *The Occident* could have become forums for a philosophical or theological debate on the issue of feminism, but that did not happen. Nor were the serialized stories so popular with the readers, especially of Wise's German language *Deborah,* used to further the cause of feminism

RESPONSA BY COMMITTEE

Yet the pendulum did not swing in only one direction, for Kaufmann Kohler felt the need for a solid basis in tradition for specific questions that rabbinic colleagues raised and in 1906 established the Responsa Committee of the Central Conference of American Rabbis.[58] Soon some responsa were published in its Yearbooks along with the report of the committee. The very fact of creating responsa through a committee rather than through a single scholar was novel and a bow to the democratic impulse. The Conference rarely turned to the committee for halakhic guidance, however, before debating and adopting major matters. So, for example, my long responsum on patrilineal descent was written after the decision had been made. In other words, this older method of reaching decisions continued for many practical matters of daily life that concerned both the rabbis and the congregants but was generally not used by committee chairs or the broader Conference as a body.

A major exception to this was the question of women's ordination as the Conference sought the advice from the chair of the Responsa Committee; the issue had been raised at the College in 1921 as Martha Neumark, the candidate asked to be assigned a high holiday pulpit as a student rabbi. She narrowly received a positive vote from the faculty with Kaufmann Kohler, the President of the College, breaking the tie. Kohler then turned to the Board of Governors to consider the broader question of ordination.[59] At the same time Professor Jacob Lauterbach of the College (1873–1942) was asked by the Conference to prepare and present a responsum. It came to a negative conclusion.[60] Lauterbach was not inclined to "creative misreadings of the *halakhah*." He based his decision on the principle that women are not empowered to "render decisions in ritual or religious matters" and equated the rabbi with *dayan*, citing that the ordination states *yoreh, yore, yadin, yadin* (*Yerushalmi* San 21c; Shev. 35 b; *Yad.* Hil. Sanhedrin 2.7; *Tur* and *Shulhan Arukh*, Hoshen Mishpat 7.3). In the matter of acting as a teacher, the tradition imposed some restrictions on women but generally permitted it. Lauterbach then continued by asking whether the Reform movement should separate itself from the rabbinic tradition and ordain women. He declined to do so, as in his view it would jeopardize the authority of all Reform rabbis. Furthermore, he questioned the ability of women to devote themselves fully to the task alongside their other duties. The conclusion was challenged on the matter of liberal principle by a large number of rabbis on the floor of the meeting, by women who were present, and by Professor Neumark of the Hebrew Union College, who as the father of the candidate.[61] The Conference under the leadership of a special committee, headed by Henry Cohen, then took the following position:

> Whatever may have been the specific legal status of the Jewish woman regarding certain religious function, the general position in Jewish religious life has ever been an exalted one. She has been the priestess in the home, and our sages have recognized her as the preserver of Israel. In view of these Jewish teachings and in keeping with the spirit of our age and the traditions of this conference, we declare that woman cannot justly be denied the privilege of ordination.[62]

Professor Lauterbach reluctantly modified his views under practical pressure. However, the Board of Governors refused to permit the ordination women. Neither the faculty nor the Conference was willing to push further, nor did anyone come forward and offer private ordination.[63] This demonstrated either a failure of nerve or a lack of broader interest in this issue. Although women had studied at HUC and received a Bachelor's Degree, none were ordained or pushed hard in that direction.[64] No male rabbis stepped forward to provide private ordination as did Max Dienemann (1873–1939) who ordained Regina Jonas in Berlin in 1935 almost four years after she had fulfilled all the requirements of the *Hochschule für die Wissenschaft des Judentums* (1870–1942), the liberal German rabbinic seminary. Leo Baeck added his signature to the ordination in 1941. Regina Jonas, after some difficulties, served the Berlin community until her deportation first to Theresienstadt (1942) and then to her death in Auschwitz (1944).[65]

Jonas had written a halalkhic thesis with the title"Can a Woman Hold Rabbinical Office" for Professor Baneth who was to ordain. He regarded it as "good." This could have been the basis of a responsum, but remained unknown.[66]

The question of ordination was revisited by the Central Conference in 1956 with the approval of Nelson Glueck, the president of the Hebrew Union College. However this did not lead to a positive resolution.[67] Subsequently there were resolutions by the National Federation of Temple Sisterhoods, but no follow through by them; an Emma Goldman was lacking.

We should note that the simple path of innovation first taken by Israel Jacobson, and Max Dienemann finally resolved the issue of women's ordination in North America and largely in the same way. It was a unilateral decision taken with little internal or institutional discussion by Nelson Glueck, President of the Hebrew Union College, who admitted Sally Prisant or Alfred Gottschalk, his successor, who ordained her in 1972. There was no debate at the Central Conference, by the Board of Governors of the College or the Union of American

Hebrew Congregations (which passed a congratulatory resolution),[68] nor any question addressed to the Responsa Committee. This innovation was accepted, perhaps reluctantly by some, but without major protest.

With this question and others responsa here faced the democratic impulse. The Central Conference had wished to anchor this significant step in the Tradition, but that did not prove possible. The responsa committee holds a special position in the Conference. It is part of this democratic organization and in theory a committee like all others. In practice, however, it remains distinctive. Until my time as chairman, the committee never met and was rarely consulted as the chairman answered all questions and spoke for the committee. I introduced the practice of regular meetings and consultation on the major questions asked, yet ultimately, wrote the reponsa. That remains the current practice. Responsa continue to be used to inform both the rabbinate and the broader public but are not binding upon them.

Responsa continues to be a potential path toward change, but more as a way of justifying innovation. They began to be used systematically and in a broader manner in the early 1950s through the efforts of Solomon B. Freehof (1892-1990) as chair of the Responsa Committee. His *Reform Jewish Practice and Its Rabbinic Background* took a further step in placing contemporary practice into a traditional context. As questions began to be directed to him, he wrote formal responsa, reopening this path for innovation and justifying it. Freehof understood that there was opposition to this voice of authority and stated that these decisions represented "guidance not governance" which was his way of avoiding conflict. Because Freehof's responsa were published by the Hebrew Union College Press they had additional status.

Freehof's effort, at least in theory, represented a combination of the older style of responsa, i.e. produced by a single individual and the pattern sought by the Conference of working with a committee, which he partially followed. A collection of the responsa issued by the Committee and published by the Conference, albeit in mimeographed form, may have represented at least a semi-conscious objection to Freehof's style of going it alone.[69] This slim volume was another indication that the path of responsa in an advisory role would be taken more seriously. Yet they remained either advisory or provided traditional grounding after a significant resolution had been passed. That was the case with "Patrilineal Descent." The Resolution was adopted in March,1983 and I was a member of that committee. The rabbinic tradition had been thoroughly discussed in the committee proceedings and was mentioned in the committee report. The committee, however, did not request a responsumas part of its report. My responsum on the subject was not issued till October 1983.[70]

I took the role of the committee seriously and under my chairmanship the Responsa Committee undertook the task of reviewing the existing responsa of the Conference and adding material that brought them in line with contemporary thought. That volume was published by the Conference. This step, somewhat akin to the older halakhic process of adding commentary to an existing work. Responsa now were more than a few pages in the *Yearbook* and became more important in the individual decisions of rabbis and congregants. Significant new questions were asked in greater numbers; As not all could be discussed without endless delay for those who had asked the question, only the most significant were subject to committee discussion and the decisions represented the committee. Aside from preparing a text to which the committee could respond and make its suggestions, my main task was two-fold. I sought to avoid minority opinions as those who asked sought an answer, not a choice. Secondly the answer while perhaps containing some compromise due to the committee process, still needed to be firm with a specific direction. These responsa and others which I gave outside the committee process made responsa more important to the Reform

Jewish community as well as the Central Conference. My two additional volumes of responsa were published by the Conference in succeeding years.[71] A more recent volume under the leadership of Mark Washofsky followed.[72] In 1990 the newly established Solomon B. Freehof Institute for Progressive *Halakhah*, which I founded along with Moshe Zemer, have brought halahkhic views on a wide variety of contemporary issues to the broader Jewish public. They also continue a more democratic and open approach as they do not seek to provide a single answer to the issues discussed, but represent a range of scholarly opinions. This effort will not replace responsa as those who ask specific questions seek an answer, not essays. The sixteen volumes of halakhic essays and responsa thus far published continue to provide a forum for *halakhah* in the Reform decision making process.[73] These volumes and symposia have dealt with a very wide range of topics from birth control and conversion to war and terrorism with essays by dozens of colleagues and academics.

These paths of responsa and halakhic studies represent an effort to include the tradition in a systematic but non-binding way in the structure of the Central Conference. The Pittsburgh statement of 1999 indicates a greater bond with the tradition. This older path continues to be part of the mechanism of change. Yet it has been clothed in the garb of democracy and so functions within those limits.

Some Conclusions

Let us begin with feminism. While change in some areas came swiftly, in others it was surprisingly slow. Despite the series of questions on women which Napoleon asked, none of the Jewish responses even hinted that progress for women was necessary and a logical step in the emancipation of all Jews.

In the early nineteenth century progress in young women's education came slowly with small steps taken in a number of cities.

Upper class individuals had already begun the process privately half a century earlier. Governmental policies forced changes in Jewish education, but only for males. The writings of Pestalozzi and those influenced by him stimulated feminine education and in the second half of the century this included the Orthodox world

The steps taken by the three mid-century rabbinic conferences made substantial changes and went further that the surrounding Christian world. They were, however, caught up in an internal battle over traditional justification for such changes versus a simple declaration that modern Judaism is different and need not heed tradition. That struggle did not halt the process, however, but it stopped short of a full declaration of equality. The last convention was willing to have such a statement placed on the table but then referred it to a future meeting. No one at the future meetings in Germany or North America was willing to reintroduce it.

From 1848 on German Jews spent their effort fighting for equal rights for men and so dodged the issue. In North America where this was not as issue, it was simply avoided even when introduced by someone as prominent as Kaufmann Kohler. That continued to be the pattern even while women's suffrage was widely debated in the broader world. Even after the victory of the suffrage movement the reluctance to ordain a woman remained.

After the initial burst of enthusiastic liberalism, the organized Reform movement lost interest in feminism and whatever progress was made came through the *minhag* or the action of a single individual. The stand on feminism represents a very mixed record until the social justice movement of the 1960s and beyond.

Now let us turn to the mechanism of change. The Jewish communities since Napoleon's Sanhedrin of 1807 have worked out a series of parallel mechanisms for innovation to meet the conditions of modern life. The community reconstituted itself and began a struggle for full civil rights while it continued to make numerous changes.

Six mechanisms of change have existed in a parallel fashion, each with a claim to authority but in reality sharing such authority, even if unwillingly or silently. The most widely accepted mechanism was the democratic assembly in which the members or their delegates debated and then settled issues through the vote. This has been widely accepted by the entire Jewish world, though frequently it is not sufficiently decisive.

Equally significant was the independent democratic voice of the people as expressed in the creation of *minhagim*. They were shaped without discussion and were simply accepted, often against the opposition of portions of the leadership, both lay and rabbinic, yet they have overcome that challenge more frequently than in the past.

Change based upon the notion of historical development and intellectual justification through pointing to similar steps taken in the past have always had a strong intellectual appeal. Initially this came under the heading of progress, but we might better see it as rising to the challenge of new conditions not necessarily representing an improvement on the past.

As new Jewish theologies and philosophies appear, they are seen both as paths to change and ways of systematizing it so that it can be viewed in a broader fashion. The various Reform platforms have used this method, yet only the first Pittsburgh Platform (1885), although officially adopted by no one, captured the essence of the Reform movement from a philosophical perspective. Perhaps its success lay in the fact that it was not the work of a committee, but of a single mind.

Innovation through an authoritative voice, responsa in Judaism, represents the oldest method . It justifies or rejects an action,. This was widely used initially, but failed as too conservative, too slow and too mired in the past. Furthermore it depended on personal authority, often rejected in the name of personal autonomy. Reborn as the function of a committee, it has a bright future as it combines the voices of democracy with those of authority.

Innovation created by a gifted charismatic leader acting entirely alone has always been important, frequently within the halakhic framework. In the modern period it proved to be most useful at the beginning whether through Israel Jacobson in Germany or Isaac Mayer Wise in America. After the community had reconstructed itself and established other avenues, it played a smaller role. In the contemporary highly organized Jewish world it is a less likely to be as effective as in the past.

Through each of these ways modern Jewish life has been reconstructed and established on a firm footing in all the lands where Jews now reside. The community is vastly different from that of the eighteenth century, yet in many ways stronger and more resilient. The unsettled atmosphere of the early nineteenth century gave way with surprising rapidity to new forms of organization. It created contemporary voluntary world in which Judaism depends entirely on internal discipline along with perhaps social pressure, as no external mechanisms are available. Personal autonomy works for some but community demands voluntary discipline. This can be and is established through any and all of the mechanisms that have evolved. They have created a new type of Jewish community that functions in an entirely different manner. It forms a continuum with the past despite the extraordinary differences. Judaism is narrower as many traditional tasks and functions belong to the nation states in which we reside this includes Israel which has constituted itself like other nation states. Within those parameters Jewish life has not only flourished, but found ways to expand the influence of our religious and ethical message in the world.

Notes

1. Moses Sofer, *Responsa Orah Hayyim*, 28, 181; *Yoreh Deah* 19, etc. See the discussion in Eliezer Katz, *Hatam Sofer – His Life and Work*, Jerusalem, 1969 (Hebrew). See also note 11.

2. See Walter Jacob, "The Woman in Reform Judaism – Meeting or Avoiding the Issue" W. Jacob (ed.) *Gender Issues in Jewish Law – Essays and Responsa,* Pittsburgh, 2002, pp. 130 ff. For the 19th century background of feminist struggles see Bonnie S. Anderson and Judith P. Zinsser, *A History of Their Own – Women in Europe from Prehistory to the Present*, New York, 1988, Vol. 2; Susan M. Okin, *Women in Western Political Thought*, Princeton, 1979; Catherine Clinton, *The Other Civil War - American Women in the Nineteenth Century*, New York, 1984; Ellen Carol DuBois, *Feminism and Suffrage: The Emergence of an Independent Women's Movement in America 1848– 1869*, Ithica N.Y., 1978; Joan Hoff, *Law, Gender, and Justice – A Legal History of U.S. Women*, New York, 1991; Mary Ritter Beard, *Women as a Force in History: A Study in Traditions and Realities*, New York, 1946.

3. See Walter Jacob, " Napoleon's Sanhedrin and the Halakhah," in W. Jacob (ed.), *Napoleon's Influence on Jewish Law*, Pittsburgh, 2007, pp.1 ff.

4. Louis Finkelstein, *Jewish Self-Government in the Middle Ages*, New York, 1964, pp. 111 ff.; S. Baron, *The Jewish Community,* New York, 1942, Vol. 2; L. Epstein, *Marriage Laws in Bible and Talmud*, Cambridge, 1942; L. Loew, *"Eheliche Abhandlungen,: Gesammeltew Schiften*, Szegedin, 1893, Vol. 3; Ze'ev Falk, *Jewish Matrimonial Law in the Middle Ages*, Oxford,1966, pp. 13 ff.

5. See Walter Jacob in W. Jacob (ed.), *Napoleon's Influence on Jewish Law*, Pittsburgh, 2007, pp. 50 ff.

6. *Protocolle der ersten Rabbiner Versammlung abgehalten in Braunschweig*, Braunschweig, 1844.

7. Jacob R. Marcus, *Israel Jacobson*, Cincinnati, 1972, is a charming biography of this leader; this study was first published in 1928. Details of Jacobson's efforts, what influenced him and critical analyses may be found in many of the works cited in this study.

8. Little is known about the literacy of the average Jewish woman in the Middle Ages. The publication of devotional books in Judeo-German specifically addressed to women attests to some degree of literacy in northern Europe. Through the centuries a few well educated and scholarly women were mentioned. Matters changed in the eighteenth century, especially in Berlin, as the daughters of wealthy Jews received a broad secular education but little or nothing Jewish.

9. The records indicate that the school enrolled girls. Michael A. Meyer in his *Response to Modernity*, Oxford, New York, 1988, p. 39f., indicated that although the documents stated that girls were to participate in the Confirmation/graduation exercises of 1810 there is no indication that this occurred.

10. Samuel Echt, *Die Geschichte der Juden in Danzig*, 1972, in Michael Meyer, Op. Cit. p. 408.

11. Aaron Chorin, *Ein Wort zu seiner Zeit*, Vienna, 1820, p. 55.

12. Mordecai Eli*av, Jüdische Erziehung in Deutschland im Zeitalter der Aufklärung und Emanzipation*, Berlin, 2001. A more personal view is provided by some of the autobiographies in Monika Richarz, *Jüdisches Leben in Deutschland – Selbstzeugnisse zur Sozialgeschichte, 1780 – 1871*, New York, 1976.

13. Ismar Elbogen "*Jüdische Geschichte und Literatur,*" Moritz Stern, "Bibliographie" in Ludwig Geiger (ed.), *Abraham Geiger Sein Leben und Lebenswerk*, Berlin, 1910 (republished in Berlin, 2001 under the auspieces of the Abraham Geiger College); Max Wiener (ed.), *abraham geiger and liberal judaism*, Philadelphia, 1962 – especially pp. 177 ff.; Michael A. Meyer. "Abraham Geiger's Historical Judaism in Jacob Petuchowski (ed.), *New Perspectives on Abraham Geiger*, Cincinnati, 1975.

14. Abraham Geiger, *Wissenschaftliche Zeitschrift für jüdische Theologie*, Vol. 3, 1837, p. 7.

15. Mordecai Breuer, *Modernity within Tradition – A Social History of Orthodox Jewry in Imperial Germany*, New York, 1992, pp. 123 ff. Samson Raphael Hirsch emphasized the role of prospective Jewish mothers and the need to educate them

properly (*Jeshurun,* 1862, pp. 417 ff.). Hirsch's school in Frankfurt even had mixed classes until the growing enrollment permitted gender separation. The Orthodox Israel Salanter (1819–1883) on visiting Hildesheimer in Berlin noted that he lectured to young women, which would have led to an uproar in Lithuania (Ibid. 125). See also J. Carlebach, "Family Structure and the Position of Jewish Women," in W. Mosse, *Revolution and Evolution–1848 in German Jewish History,* Tuebingen, 1981.

16. Alexander Altmann, *Moses Mendelssohn, A Biographical Study,* Philadelphia, 1973, p. 382; Moses Sofer's concerns were limited, but were expanded into an absolute prohibition by his descendants and disciples in keeping with the separatist later mood. Sofer himself was much more nuanced; his children learned German and approved a proposal for a seminary which taught secular subjects, etc. Meir Hildesheimer, "The Attitude of the Hatam Sofer Toward Moses Mendelssohn," *Academy for Jewish Research,* 1994, Vol. 60. pp. 141–188; Meir Hildesheimer, "The Secular Language and Secular Studies – Attitudes toward Them in the Thought of the Hatam Sofer and his Disciples," *Academy for Jewish Research,* Vol. 62, 1996, Jerusalem, 1996, pp. 129–164.

17. Mordecai Eliav, *Op. Cit.,* p. 20.

18. A series of articles by Abraham Geiger , *Wissenschaftliche Zeitschrift für jüdische Theologie,* Frankfurt a.M., 1835, Vol. 1 and subsequent volumes. Some have been republished in Ludwig Geiger (ed.), *Nachgelassene Schriften.*

19. More recent studies do not bear thisconclusion out.

20. A. Geiger, "*Die Stellung des weiblichen Geschlechtes in dem Judentume unserer Zeit,*" *Wissenschaftliche Zeitschrift für jüdische Theologie,* Vol. 3, 1837, pp. 10 ff.

21. Ibid., p. 18ff.

22. *Nogah Hatzedek,* Dessau, 1818; Eliezer Lieberman, *Or Hanogah,* Dessau, 1818, were followed by Orthodox attacks in *Eleh Divrei Habrit,* Altona, 1819, Abraham Loewenstamm, *Tzeror Hahayyim,* Amsterdam 1821 and others. Much later German responsa of twelve rabbis defended the changes of the Hamburg prayer book in *Theologische Gutachten über das Gebetbuch des Neuen Israelitischen Tempelvereins in Hamburg,* Hamburg, 1842; and a later broader defense through *Rabbinische Gutachten über die Vertreglichkeit der freien Forschung mit dem Rabbineramt,* 1843. A year later Rabbi Solomon Abraham

Trier assembled a series of German language responsa from Orthodox rabbis defending circumcision in the volume *Rabbinische Gutachten über die Beschneidung* (Frankfurt a. M., 1844). This was part of the struggle against a radical Reform group that sought to eliminate circumcision. This Orthodox effort in the vernacular was not repeated.

23. Michael Meyer, *Op. Cit.,* pp. 122 ff.

24. See Walter Jacob, "Solomon B. Freehof and the Halachah – An Appreciation," in Solomon B. Freehof, *Reform Responsa for our Time,* Cincinnati, 1977, p. xv.

25. Abraham Geiger, *Wissenschaftliche Zeitschrift,* 1837, Vol. 3, p. 7.

26. Jacob Petuchowski, *Prayerbook Reform in Europe,* New York, 1968.

27. David Novak, *Law and Theology in Judaism,* New York, 1974, Vol. 1, 2.

28. For details of Geiger's intentions, see Ludwig Geiger, *Abraham Geiger, Leben und Lebenswerk,* Berlin, 1910, pp. 114 ff. Other forces were at work too. First the statements of the radical *Reform Verein* of Frankfurt which had made strong statements on the abrogation of *brit milah* and intermarriage. These had to be confronted. In addition many professional groups were organizing on a regional or national basis in order to gain strength, consult with each other, and come to common decisions. See Michael Meyer, *Response to Modernity – A History of the Reform Movement in Judaism,* New York,1988, p. 427, note 125.

29. The rabbis that attended the Conferences are listed; others were present, but not in an official capacity and were not named:

BRUNSWICK CONFERENCE June 12–19, 1844
WORMS - A Adler. ALZEY - S. Adler   COBLENZ - Ben Israel
HILDESHEIM - Bodenheimer MINDEN - Adler, OFFENBACH - Formstecher
HAMBURG -   Frankfurter BRESLAU - Geiger KURHESSEN - Goldman
SONDERHAUSEN - Heidenheim BRUNSWICK - Herzfeld
BERNBURG -   Herxheimer WEIMAR - Hess LUXENBURG - Hirsch
MEININGEN - Hoffmann MECKLENBURG-SCHWERIN - Holdheim
MANESWERDER - Jolowicz TREVES - J. Kahn POMERANIA - Klein
STUTTGART - Maier (was president of the Conference)
MAGDEBURG - Philippson HAMBURG - Salomon, Randegg: Schott
BINGEN - Soberheim

FRANFURT-ON-THE MAIN CONFERENCE July 15–28, 1845
FRANKFURT a.M. - J. Auerbach, BIRKENFELD - Einhorn
DRESDEN - Frankel MARBURG - Gosen BUCHAU - Gueldenstein
FRANKFORT - Jost ALT-BREISACH - Reiss BURGKUNSTADT - Stein
WIESBADEN- : Suesskind WEIBURG - Treuenfels MANNHEIM - Wagner
OLDENBURG - Wechsler FRANKFURT a.M.. - Leopold Stein (as President of
the Conference)

BRESLAU CONFERENCE July 13–24, 1846

WORMS - A. Adler ALZEY - S. Adler, FRANKFURT a.M. - J. Auerbach
COBLENZ - : Ben Israel BIRKENFELD - Einhorn OFFENBACH - Formstecher
BRESLAU - Geiger (who was president of the conference) WAREN - Goldstein
MARBURG - Gosen BUCHAU- Gueldenstein, BERNBURG - Herxheimer
BRUNSWICK - Herzfeld EISENACH - Hess,
MECKLENBURG-SCHWERIN - Holdheim TREVES - J. Kahn
BRESLAU - M. Levy MÜNSTERBERG - L. Loevy TEPLITZ - Pick
MAGDEBURG - Philippson BINGEN - Sobernheim FRANKFURT A.m. - Stein
MANNHEIM - Wagner OLDENBURG - Wechsler

30. Some rabbis were not permitted to attend by their governments. Ultimately the Orthodox objected vigorously to the decisions made and gathered signatures of colleagues from neighboring lands. Heinrich Graetz, *Geschichte der Juden*, Leipzig, 1878 , Vol. 11, p. 534. See also .*I.M.* Jost, *Geschichte.*des Judenthums und seiner Sekten, Leipzig, 1859, Vol. 3, pp. 379 ff.

31. Louis Finkelstein, *Jewish Self-Government in the Middle Ages*, New York, 1964; Salo Wittmayer Baron, *The Jewish Community*, Philadelphia, 1945; Y. Baer, "The Foundations and Beginnings of Jewish Organizations in the Middle Ages," *Zion*, Vol. 25, 1940; A. Agus, "The Autonomous Rule of the Jewish Communities in the Middle Ages," *Talpiot*, 1951, Vol. 5; S. Dubnow, *Pinkas Hamedinah*, Jerusalem 1969; Samuel Atlas, "The General Will in Talmudic Jurisprudence," *Hebrew Union College Annual*, Vol. 26, 1955, pp. 1 – 38. Records of such councils have not survived.

32. Let us take a brief look at the special function of the ancient great Sanhedrin. The origins and the way in which the ancient great Sanhedrin functioned are not clear as the various sources contradict each other. This Sanhedrin as a religious and political institution seems to have functioned through the Hellenistic period, with its membership changing to reflect the struggle between Saducees and Pharisees. Echoes of these struggles appear in the *Mishnah, Tosefta,* the *Babli* and *Jerushalmi,*

Josephus, and the *New Testament* as well as the Dead Sea Scrolls. It was viewed as the ultimate religious authority. Long after it had ceased to function, an idealized version of its procedures was described in the mishnaic literature. We cannot judge the accuracy of this description.

Maimonides provided a description of its powers and functions as he understood them: It had the power to make major decisions that were to be recognized by all and could do so by majority vote. .Membership in this august body was limited to those that had received ordination in the continuous line that according to tradition traced itself to Moses. However, when the Great Assembly turned to the qualifications for membership, they agreed that there were no specifications, voted on the matter and settled it. As ordination in the traditional sense stopped in the fourth century, it meant that this route for making changes or modifications in the *halakhah* were no longer available.

The need for greater flexibility was felt from time to time, but no one was sufficiently bold to attempt the reintroduction of ordination and thus to begin the process of recreating a Great Sanhedrin. The exception was Jacob Berab of Safed. In the sixteenth century made the bold attempt which immediately failed since he did not include the leading rabbinic authority of Jerusalem. This effort would undoubtedly have collapsed anyhow a bit later. Those that participated in this venture, such as Joseph Karo, did not mention it in their writings as it would only have injured their reputation. No subsequent similar efforts to create a central Jewish religious authority that might have the power to make major changes in the *halakhah* were undertaken.

33. "Statuten," *Protocolle, Op. Cit.*, xii ff.

34. *Protocolle und Aktenstuecke der zweiten Rabbiner Versammlung abgehalten in Frankfurt am Main*, Frankfurt, 1845. Frankel left after a debate on the report of a commission that suggested that Hebrew be limited to *barkhu*, the following paragraphs, *shema* and its paragraphs, the initial three and final three paragraphs of the *amidah*, and the Torah reading. The remainder of the service could be in the vernacular [German] (p. 61). There was considerable discussion; the vote on this issue was for acceptance of the report eighteen to twelve, with Frankel not participating. He then immediately published a statement declaring his objection (p. 72). This statement was brought to the attention of the Conference two days later and the assembly decided against publishing a rejoinder and starting a public polemic against him (pp. 86 ff.) Although this was the ostensible reason for Frankel's withdrawal, his theological position differed on many other matters with the majority in attendance.

Frankel also expounded a historical view of the tradition but limited himself to the post-biblical period. His works *Ueber den Einfluss der palaestinischen Exegese auf die alexandrinische Hermeneutik*, Leipzig 1851 and his *Darkhei Hamishnah*, Leipzig, 1859 provided a historical, critical approach to these classic texts.

35. I.M. Jost, *Geschichte des Judenthums und seiner Sekten*, Leipzig, 1859, Vol. 3, pp. 379 ff. Jost as a contemporary followed the proceedings closely.

36. A. Geiger, *"Die Stellung des weiblichen Geschlechtes in dem Judentume unserer Zeit" Wissenschaftliche Zeitschrift fuer jüdische Theologie,* Vol. 3, 1837, pp. 10 ff.

37. Adler's paper is reprinted as an appendix to this volume as it is not generally available.

38. *Protokolle der dritten Versammlung deutscher Rabbiner*, Breslau, 1847, pp. 253.

39. *Ibid.*, 1847, p. 265.

40. Samuel Holdheim's response appeared in *Die religiöse Stellung des weiblichen Geschlechtes im talmudischen Judenthum,* Schwerin, 1846, 79 pp.; *Die Erste Rabbinerversammlung und Herr Dr. Frankel,* Schwerin, 1845, 35 pp.; see also Philipson, *The Reform Movement in Judaism*, Cincinnati, 1930, p. 145

41. Sefton D. Temkin, *The New World of Reform Containing the Proceedings of the Conference of Reform Rabbis Held in Philadelphia in November 1869 – Translated from the German with an Introduction and Notes,* Bridgeport, 1974, viii, 123 pp.

42. *Yearbook of the Central Conference of American Rabbis*, 1892–93, Cincinnati, 1893, p. 40.

43. Dr. Max Landsberg, "The Position of Women and the Jews," pp. 241–254 and Henrietta SzoldJosephine Lazarus, "What has Judaism done for Woman," pp. 304–310, *Judaism at the World's Parliament of Religions*, Cincinnati, 1894. Josephine Lazarus also presented a paper, but not on this topic.

44. This meeting led to the call for a National Council of Jewish Women in 1894, which was more concerned with charitable efforts than women's suffrage initially.

45. *Yearbook of the Central Conference of American Rabbis,* Cincinnati, Vol. 23, p. 120, 1914. "Resolution on Woman Suffrage" proposed for 1913 national convention, signed by Moses P. Jacobson, Harry H. Mayer, G. Deutsch, Wm. S., Friedman, Harry Weiss, Isaac Rypins. For the rejection see p. 133.

46. *Yearbook of the Central Conference of American Rabbis,* Cincinnati, Vol. 25, Convention 1915, Cincinnati, 1915, p. 133.

47. *Yearbook of the Central Conference of American Rabbis,* Cincinnati, Vol. 27, 1917, pp.

48. This is not a complete list, but a sampling: White Slave Trade (1911), Wage Discrimination (1963), Rabbinic Family Relationships (1975), Women on the Board of Trustees (1976), Affirmative Action (1978), Patrilineal Descent (1983), Economic Justice for Women (1983), Jewish Day Care (1984), Violence Against Women (1990), Women's Health Care (1992), Abuse in the Family (1992), Women's Health (1993),Women in Professional Life (1993), Reproductive Rights Life (1993), International Women's Rights (1994), Breast Cancer (1997), Women's Rights (2008).

49. For their current legislative agenda on women's issues see their website www.Social Action Center of Reform Judaism.org

50. The Women's Rabbinic Network created in 1975 as a constituent of the Central Conference of America Rabbis continues to guide and strengthen women in the rabbinate and to deal with feminine issues.

51. James G. Heller, *Isaac M. Wise – His Life, Work and Thought,* New York, 1965, pp 213.

52. *Ibid.,* pp. 568 ff. Wise mentions it casually in the introduction to his *Minhag America.,* which gave this newly established *minhag* broad publicity.

53. Eleanor Flexner, *A Century of Struggle - the Women's Rights Movement in the United States,* New York, Atheneum, 1973, p. 143 ff.

54. For a contemporary discussion see Mark Washofsky , "Minhag and Halakhah," in Walter Jacob and Moshe Zemer (eds.), *Rabbinic - Lay Relations in Jewish Law,* Pittsburgh, 1993, pp. 99 ff.

55. For a discussion of the Pittsburgh Platform see Walter Jacob, (ed.,) *The Changing World of Reform Judaism – Pittsburgh Platform in Retrospect.*, Pittsburgh, 1985, pp. 104 ff. The full text of the meeting has been reproduced there. Also Sefton D. Temkin, "The Pittsburgh Platform – A Centennial Assesment," *Journal of Reform Judaism*, Fall 1985, Vol. 32, No. 4, pp.1 ff.; Dana E. Kaplan (ed.), *Platforms and Prayer Books*, New York, 2002.

56. This is the complete text of Kaufmann Kohler's statement:

PLATFORM

Dr. Kohler laid the following platform before the Conference for its consideration:

In view of the wide divergence of opinions and the conflicting ideas prevailing in Judaism today to such an extent as to cause alarm and feeling of uncertainty among our well-meaning coreligionists and an appalling religious indifference and lethargy among the masses, we, as representatives of Reform Judaism, here unite upon the following principles:

1. While discerning in every religion a human attempt to grasp the Infinite and Omnipotent One and in every sacred form, source and book of revelation offered by any religious system the consciousness of the indwelling of God in man, we recognize in Judaism the highest conception of God and of His relation to man - expressed as the innate belief of man in the One and holy God, the Maker and Ruler of the World, the King, the Father and Educator of the Human Race, represented in Holy Scriptures as the faith implanted into the heart of the original man and arrived at in all the cheering brightness by the forefathers, the inspired prophets, singers and writers of Israel, developed and ever more deepened and spiritualized into the highest moral progress of their respective ages and under continual struggles and trials, defended and preserved by the Jewish people as the highest treasure of the human race.

2. We prize and treasure the books comprising the national library of Israel preserved under the name of Holy Scriptures, as the records of Divine Revelation and of the consecration of the Jewish people of this mission as priests of the one God; but we consider their composition, their arrangements and their entire contents as the work of men, betraying in their conceptions of the world of shortcomings of their age.

3. While finding in the miraculous narratives of the Bible childlike conceptions of the dealing of Divine love and justice with man, we today, in common with many Jewish thinkers of the Spanish era, welcome the results of natural science and progressive research in all fields of life as the best help to

understand the working of the Divine Love, the Bible serving us as guide to find the Divine power working from within.

4. Beholding in the Mosaic Laws a system of training of the Jewish people for its mission as a nation among the nations of antiquity, planted upon the soil of Palestine, we accept only the moral laws and statutes as a divine, but reject all those social, political and priestly statutes which are in no way shape and form adapted to our mode of life and to our views and habits as people scattered among the nations of the globe, and standing upon the level of a far higher culture of mind and heart than stood the people for whom they are intended.

5. All the Mosaic Rabbinical Laws on diet, priestly purity and dress, originating in ages and under associations of ideas altogether foreign to our mental and spiritual state, do no longer impress us with the character of divine institutions, and fail to imbue us with the spirit of priestly holiness, their observance in our day being apt to obstruct rather than enhance and encourage our moral and spiritual elevation as children of God.

6. While glorying in our great past with its matchless history of one continued wondrous struggle and martyrdom in the defense of the Unity of God, which necessitated the exclusion of the Jewish people from a world stamped with polytheism and idolatry, with all their cruelty and vice, we hail in the modern era of universal culture of heart and mind the approaching realization of Israel's great Messianic hope for the kingdom of peace, truth, justice and love among all men, expecting neither a return to Palestine, nor the restitution of any of the laws concerning a Jewish State, nor a sacrificial worship under the administration of the sons of Aaron.

7. We behold in Judaism an ever-growing, progressive and rational religion, one which gave rise to the religions which today rule the greater part of the civilized globe. We are convinced of the utmost necessity of preserving our identity with our great past; we gladly recognize in the spirit of broad humanity and cosmopolitan philanthropy permeating our age, in the noble and grand endeavor to widen and deepen the idea and to enlarge the dominion of man, our best ally and help in the fulfillment of our mission and the only means of achieving the end aim of our religion.

8. We therefore hail with the utmost delight and in the spirit of sincere fellowship and friendship the efforts on the part of the representatives of the various religious denominations the world over, and particularly in our free country, toward removing the barriers separating men from men, class from class, and sect from sect, in order to cause each to grasp the hands of his fellow-men and thus form one great brotherhood of men on earth. In this growing religion of humanity, based upon the belief in one God as Father of men, and the conception of man as the image of God we find the working of the Divine plan of truth and salvation as revealed through Jewish history.

9. In view of the Messianic end and object of Jewish history, we feel bound to do our utmost to make our religious truth and our sacred mission understood to all and appreciated by all, whether Jew or Gentile; to improve and reform our religious forms and habits of life so as to render them expressive of the great cosmopolitan ideas pervading Judaism and to bring about the fulfillment of the great prophetic hope and promise "that the house of God should be the house of prayer for all nations."

10. Seeing in the present crisis simply the natural consequences of a transition from a state of blind authority – belief and exclusion – to a rational grasp and humanitarian conception and practice of religion, we consider it a matter of the utmost necessity to organize a Jewish mission for the purpose of enlightening the masses about the history and the mission of the Jewish people and elevating their social and spiritual condition through press, pulpit and school.

57. Walter Jacob (ed.), *The Changing World of Reform Judaism – The Pittsburgh Platform in Retrospect.*

58. Walter Jacob (ed.), *American Reform Responsa*, New York, 1983, p. xvi.

59. The Board of the College could not make up its mind originally and so asked for a faculty opinion in spring of 1921. Lauterbach, although opposed , reluctantly proposed that women be ordained as "Reform Judaism has in many other instances departed from traditional practice...." In the summer Lauterbach read his reponsum to the convention of the Central Conference; following a heated discussion , the convention voted fifty-six to eleven for the ordination of women. The matter then came back to the Board of Governors of the College in February of 1923 and despite the faculty and Rabbinic vote decided against ordination. See Michael A.Meyer, "A Centennial History," in Samuel Karff (ed.), *Hebrew Union College-Jewish Institute of Religion at One Hundred Years*, Cincinnati, 1976.

60. The issue could have been raised earlier in North America by Isaac Mayer Wise who was willing to admit women to study for the rabbinate. Heller, *Isaac Mayer Wise, His Life, Work, and Thought*, New York, 1965, p. 571.

61. *Yearbook of the Central Conference of American Rabbis*, Cincinnati, 1922, pp. 156 ff.

62. *Ibid.* pp. 24 ff.; *Yearbook of the Central Conference of American Rabbis*, Cincinnati, 1922, pp. 156 ff. This brief statement in favor of the ordination of women was issued by a special committee following the discussion of Lauterbach's responsum.

63. Ellen Uimansky in her analysis of this issue wrote that Lauterbach, at the conclusion of a lengthy discussion at a Board of Governors meeting of the Hebrew Union College, reluctantly agreed that as Reform Judaism has departed from the tradition in many ways, it cannot logically refuse the ordination of women. (Ellen Umansky, "Women's Journey toward Rabbinic Ordination," in Gary P. Zola (ed,) *Women Rabbis – Exploration and Celebration*, p. 32. Her documentation cites HUC correspondence. Lauterbach's final position remains unclear as he did not withdraw his responsum. Also in 1922 The Jewish-Institute-of -Religion founded by Stephen Wise in New York admitted Irma Levy Lindheim as a rabbinic candidate, but she was not able to complete her studies.

64. Other led congregational services after some self-study; the best known among them was Ray Frank. For more on her and others, see Ellen Umansky, *Ibid.* and Gary P. Zola, "Twenty Years if Women in the Rabbinate," G. Zola (ed.) *Women Rabbis - Exploration and Celebration.*

65. Rabbi Eduard Baneth , the professor who presided over ordinations, died before Ragina Jonas passed her final oral examination. His successor Chanoch Albeck refused to ordain a woman. He did not wish to be the first to do so.. This meant that no one from the faculty was willing to grant her ordination. Mostly such a refusal occurred through ideological differences. For example when my grandfather Benno Jacob had completed his studies at the *Jüdische Theologisches Seminar* in Breslau in 1887, the Seminary's ordaining rabbi refused to ordain him as he was a disciple of Heinrich Graetz, who also taught there. He and other students who were in the same position were then ordained by a special committee of the *Allgemeiner Rabbiner Verband.*

Jonas' path to ordination has been described in Elisa Klapheck (ed.), *Fraülein Rabbiner Jonas,* Teetz, 2000, pp. 38 ff. This book also published Jonas' paper "Can a Woman Become Rabbi" (German). For more on women in the *Hochschule für die Wissenschaft des Judenthums*, see Esther Seidel, *Women Pioneers of Jewish Learning,* Berlin, 2002; Katharina von Kellenbach, "God Does Not Oppress Any Humand Being: The Life And Thought of Rabbi Regina Jonas," *Leo Baeck Year-Book*, New York, 1994, Vol. 39; Alexander Guttmann, "The Woman Rabbi: An Historical Perspective," *Journal of Reform Judaism*, Summer, 1982, Vol. 29, Nu. 3, pp. 21ff.

66. See Katharina von Kellenbach's essay. I have not yet had an opportunity to study Jonas' thesis, but plan to make it available.

67. A committee under the leadership of Barnett Brickner was appointed by of the *Central Conference of American Rabbis* in 1956 to look into this matter further; it favored ordination. This step was endorsed by Nelson Glueck, the President of HUC-JIR, but the Conference tabled the report of the committee. The details of this long institutional struggle have been described in several essays in Gary P. Zola (ed.), *Women Rabbis – Exploration and Celebration*, Cincinnati, 1996, 135 pp.

68. Gary P. Zola (ed.), *Women Rabbis – Exploration and Celebration*, Cincinnati, 1996, 135 pp. For the resolution of the Board of Trustees of the Union of American Hebrew Congregations from their December 1976 meeting, see http://urj.org/Articles/index.cfm?id=7442&page_prg_id=29601&pge_id=4590 The Conservative Movement reluctantly eventually took the same step.

69. Jacob D. Schwartz (ed.), *Responsa of the Central Conference of American Rabbis*, New York, 1954 (mimeograph by the Union of American Hebrew Congregations). Freehof did not involve the Reponsa Committee at all with the exception of an annual postcard enclosed with the responsum he wished to print in the *Yearbook of the Central Conference of American Rabbis* as the report of the committee.

70. The Committee Report and Resolution were first published as an appendix to Walter Jacob (ed.), *American Reform Responsa*, New York, 1983, pp. 547 ff. The responsum on this topic, although issued in 1983 was then printed in Walter Jacob, *Contemporary American Responsa*, New York, 1987, pp.61 ff.

71. For more on my approach see "Writing Responsa: A Personal Journey," Walter Jacob (ed.), *Beyond the Letter of the Law - Essays on Diversity in the Halakhah in honor of Moshe Zemer*, Pittsburgh, 2004, pp. 103–118.

72. Walter Jacob, *Contemporary American Reform Responsa*, New York, 1987, xxii, 322 pp.; Walter Jacob, *Questions and Reform Jewish Answers – New American Reform Responsa*, New York, 1992, xxvi, 443 pp.; W. Gunther Plaut and Mark Washofsky, *Teshuvot for the Nineties*, New York, 1997, xxxi, 398 pp.

73. The publications are listed in the front of this book and at www/Jewish-Law-Institute.org

JEWS AND THE "AMERICAN FUNERAL"

Ruth Langer
In Memory of Lester Herrup

Two partners in a law firm, one Christian, one Jewish, each lost a parent within a few weeks of one another after long bouts with Alzheimer's. These two lawyers graduated from the same law school, play squash together weekly, belong to the same club, and send their children to the same prep school. They consider themselves good friends. But when the Christian lawyer's mother died one Friday, the family chose the most elegant casket, gave the funeral director her most beloved clothes and jewelry and had her expertly embalmed and made up. Gathered near the open casket, the family received visits and condolences Monday and Tuesday evenings at the funeral parlor; friends and family came to say farewell, and exclaim over Mrs. X's beauty in death. The friends, colleagues, and clients of our Christian lawyer sent bowers of flowers to express their condolences. Finally, on Wednesday, the open casket funeral was held in a beautiful church; organ and professional choir performed the deceased's favorite hymns. The minister spoke of the joy of this woman's resurrection to be with God. Interment followed in the family's elegant mausoleum, prominently positioned in the suburban town's beautifully landscaped cemetery. Afterward, the family gathered at her favorite restaurant; the next day, the Christian lawyer was back at work, feeling a loss, but knowing that he had given his mother the best farewell possible according to American ideals.

The following Wednesday afternoon, the Jewish lawyer's mother died, leaving her husband a widower. While the lawyer's parents remained quite traditional Jews, the lawyer had abandoned the old-world practices of his childhood home, affiliating with the high-status Temple in town but rarely attending. He expected his mother's funeral, like his friend's, to express equivalent public statements about his role in American society. His father, however, would have none of this. His mother was taken immediately to a Jewish funeral home where early the next morning, the *hevra qadisha*, the burial society, performed the traditional *tahara*, washing her, dressing her in simple white shrouds, and placing her in an unfinished pine wood box, which they then closed. Family had rushed into town, many arriving after midnight.

The funeral, with the casket still closed, followed immediately on Thursday morning, hardly allowing the lawyer's colleagues time to rearrange their schedules. The funeral, held at the Jewish funeral home, consisted only of a few chanted Psalms and prayers, all in Hebrew. There were no candles, no flowers, no music to lighten the atmosphere. The eulogies themselves, while well-meaning, were unintelligible to non-Jews. At the cemetery, the pall bearers had to lower the coffin manually; shovels were handed around and those gathered were expected to help fill in the dusty grave. After a few more mumbled prayers, the lawyer's father went home to sit *shiva*, expecting his children to spend the following week with him mourning their loss.

The lawyer's colleagues did not know where to send their flowers; those who had come to the cemetery had dry-cleaning bills. They felt awkward making condolence calls without the presence of the deceased and hardly knew what to make of their friend's sitting on a low stool in his father's tiny dusty living room, wearing torn clothing and bedroom slippers. Feeling that he'd effectively lost his mother years ago, our lawyer found this week of formal mourning torture. He'd have to work 90- hour weeks just to catch up! And there was no way he could, as his father expected, show up in synagogue twice every day to recite *kaddish* for the next year.

This was all so incongruous with our Jewish lawyer's own world that he determined that no one in his family would be so degraded again. When he died, his funeral would be at the Temple, complete with organ music and flowers. Only the rabbi would speak.

He would either purchase a family mausoleum, or perhaps avoid it all and be cremated. Certainly, there would be no obvious dirt! Maybe there would even be a viewing, and he'd definitely be dressed like a successful lawyer!

These sorts of dissonance have not been uncommon as Jews increasingly entered the mainstream in America. In the case of death rituals, however, the sources of this dissonance are complex. Naturally, an element of assimilation is involved. As Jews have increasingly found acceptance in American (and European) society, they have looked for ways to modify religious and ethnic behaviors that set them apart.[1] But in the case of American rituals of burial and mourning, something else was happening. Just as Jews became a numerically significant community and began to move from their immigrant worlds, the American funeral was itself evolving radically, removing almost all contact with death from the domestic scene. Not only was death increasingly taking place in the hospital, but the professionalization of the funeral industry meant that preparations for funerals and funerals themselves were no longer at home, either.

Embalming, introduced large-scale in this country first as a way to transport Civil War casualties home for burial, gradually became an art-form, allowing viewing of a life-like if ostensibly "sleeping" corpse. Expensive airtight caskets and vaults that themselves would not erode could hold these embalmed bodies, purportedly protecting them from decomposition and contact with the worms and dirt that had been banished from upper-class urban lives. Alternatives like mausoleums and cremation also avoided the unpleasant dirt and worms of the traditional grave. Coherent with this, public displays of mourning, and extended post-funeral mourning largely disappeared from the American scene. These changes generated public discourse in which supporters of the changes justified the new ways as more hygienic and psychologically more sound, reducing the traumas of death. In spite of constant critiques of the commercialization of death, most Americans perceived the new ways to be progressive, modern, and ultimately, American. No wonder that many twentieth-century Jews – like Protestants and Catholics – challenged their received traditions and embraced "the American way of death."[2]

In the Jewish world, though, the question for some was not only what is more American, but what does *halakhah* permit? Elements of these new models of death rituals presented direct challenges to Jewish conceptions of *k'vod hamet*, of showing appropriate respect and honor to the deceased, as well as to traditions of equality in death and of performing *nihum avelim*, comforting the mourners, only after the funeral.[3] The available American halakhic discussions speak to this process of negotiation with American culture. Up until recent decades, they point to the ubiquitous presence of our hypothetical lawyer-type who sought to express his role in American society by integrating the public aspects of the American funeral. Reform responsa seek to validate many of the new American customs, whereas Conservative responsa initially allow many fewer, and Orthodox almost none. However, not reflected in these halakhic discussions, at least not yet, is the growing success of the advocates of Jewish tradition. Riding on the coattails of the strident public criticisms of the American funeral that began in the early 1960s,[4] American Jewish communities increasingly follow at least aspects of traditional Jewish practice. We are living in the midst of this, as yet unwritten, chapter and can only hint at it here.[5]

Our discussion, then provides a window on a piece of the history of American Jewish funeral customs, on the context from which the current situation is retreating. Our hypothetical Jewish lawyer, then, is no longer fully typical of today's American Jew. Funerals are generally public events, and those aspects that marked this pageant as not-American were those that came under question. In what follows, I survey the halakhic discussions about such public issues, relying primarily on the published responsa of Reform rabbis, especially Solomon B. Freehof and Walter Jacob,[6] the published responsa of the Committee on Jewish Law (and Standards) of the Conservative movement's Rabbinical Assembly,[7] and the *Kol Bo al Avelut* of the Columbus-based Orthodox rabbi, Leopold Greenwald.[8]

TAHARAH AND *TAKHRIKHIN*

Issues arise beginning with the very preparation of the body for the funeral. The traditional *tahara*, the ritual washing and clothing in shrouds, had been performed by dedicated burial societies since the sixteenth century,[9] either at home or in a special building in the cemetery devoted to this purpose.[10] With the emergence of funeral homes in America, Jewish funeral homes often provided a suitable space in which the burial society could prepare the deceased for burial in the traditional manner.[11] However, the American funeral challenged several aspects of this procedure. The Conservative Movement's Committee on Jewish Law established in 1938 that "the observance of the regulations concerning a simple coffin, *Takrihim* [shrouds], *taharah*, and *talit*...is in accord with established Jewish practice and should not be deviated from." In 1946 they "strenuously opposed" substituting expensive clothing for shrouds as wasteful.[12] Probably because shrouds conflicted with the American funeral's emphasis on viewing a lifelike body, American culture, Christian and Jewish, had abandoned them. This challenge to traditional custom was only exacerbated where there was no dedicated Jewish funeral home serving a community. In 1983, already in the context of the move to retrieve Jewish customs, Ben Zion Bokser recommends moving funerals from such funeral homes into the synagogue's facilities to ensure that the Jewish traditions required by the Conservative movement will indeed be followed.[13]

Reform responses to these issues probably contributed to the Conservative movement's problems. There is no discussion of *taharah* or shrouds in pre-Freehof responsa. Freehof writes in 1944 in *Reform Jewish Practice*, "The body is buried in ordinary clothes, rarely in a shroud as was the older custom."[14] He justifies the change, noting that there is no biblical precedent for shrouds. In subsequent responsa, he mentions shrouds only incidentally and raises neither objection to burial in "street garments" nor a preference one way or the other.[15] Only in 1989 does Walter Jacob answer a direct query whether a family of limited means can avoid the high cost of shrouds by burying their grandfather in "ordinary clothes." He responds that inexpensive shrouds should be obtainable; their purpose is, after all, to avoid ostentation. However "[i]t would also be permissible to use the garments which the deceased wore."[16]

Orthodox tradition of course insists on *taharah* and shrouds, but this does not insulate the communities served by orthodox rabbis from these issues. In his *Kol Bo al Avelut*, Rabbi Leopold Greenwald responds to a query from Birmingham (presumably Alabama). Here, the children of the deceased refuse to allow *taharah* and shrouds. Greenwald rules that this is not grounds for the rabbi to refuse a Jewish burial; the *taharah* is performed only to honor the deceased, and the sin is that of the children, not that of the deceased.[17] This sin, he adds, is that they are publicly decreeing that their father was wicked, for there is no requirement that one supply shrouds for the wicked. This should be the substance of the rabbinic protest against such children. If someone requests that his own burial be in something other than shrouds, however, this request is not to be honored.[18]

All sectors of the American Jewish community thus included or intersected with those desiring burial in ordinary clothes. The Orthodox reject this entirely,[19] the Conservative search for means to enforce tradition, and the Reform apparently are gradually reassessing the tradition because of the positive values it expresses.

Burial in clothing became desirable as Americans increasingly expected the deceased to appear lifelike, something that became possible with the new embalming techniques. Embalming itself raises halakhic issues, for it involves the replacement of blood with the embalming fluid that will retard or, if enough is used of the right chemicals, prevent the natural processes of decomposition. Preparing the body for display can also involve surgical procedures that traditional halakhah similarly prohibits under the category of "disfigurement" (*nivul*). In addition, Orthodox tradition also teaches that the decomposition of the body is itself a source of atonement for a person's sins. Preventing this decomposition thus has negative consequences for one's afterlife.[20] Curiously, I located no direct discussions of the permissibility of embalming in either the Reform or the Conservative responsa,[21] in spite of the fact that embalming prior to Jewish American funerals became common.[22] Also absent in these sources, apparently entirely, is any criticism of funeral directors' sale of elaborate new burial clothes.[23]

VIEWING THE DECEASED

These omissions may well be because it was easier to condemn viewings of the deceased, the primary reason for performing the embalming.[24] The Talmud establishes the prohibition on looking at the face of the deceased as one of the steps taken to ensure equality between the rich and poor in death.[25] It also suggests that looking on the face of the deceased is one of ten factors that makes learning difficult.[26] From these, traditional *halakhah* forbids uncovering or looking at the face of the deceased. Greenwald writes:

> It is obvious that the sages forbade even accidentally gazing [at the face of the deceased], and thus what they do in some places is all the more so forbidden, when they open its coffin and pass before it in procession like the gentiles do. This is a boorish act, an idolatrous

custom, and it denigrates the deceased.... Similarly,
one is not to take a photographic portrait of the
deceased to remember him by, for this involves a
possible denigration and transgression of the
prohibition of benefiting financially from the dead.[27]

Maurice Lamm gives this question extended treatment,
discussing not only the halakhic problems with viewing the dead, but
the mistaken theology and psychology that it represents, concluding:

From both viewpoints, that of Traditional Judaism and
that of psychotherapy, there is no valid reason for this
new, American, quasi-religious ceremony. On the
contrary, man, created in the image of God,
participating in the dignity of human life, deserves to
rest in peace. And the mourner deserves, at this
traumatic moment of intense grief, to be allowed to
work through, naturally and at his own pace, an
acknowledgment and an acceptance of his loss.[28]

As in our previous instances, Reform and Conservative
halakhists recognize the tradition but need to negotiate with the
overwhelming reality of the American funeral. In its earliest statement
on funerals (1938), the Rabbinical Assembly's Committee on Jewish
Law says, "Viewing of the body should be discouraged."[29] In a more
elaborate statement in 1959, it teaches, "Out of deference to Jewish
tradition with its concern for appropriate tribute to the memory of the
departed, the welfare of the family in grief, and its insistence on
safeguarding the dignity of the human being, *the practice of viewing
the deceased is to be discouraged.*" Following this, they comment on
the need for "extreme tact and patience" in dealing with families and
funeral directors to modify current customs that run counter to
halakhah. They suggest an interim step of requiring closed caskets for

the funeral itself and allowing close family and friends "the privilege of viewing the body under prescribed conditions and at specified times, prior to the funeral service."[30] In other words, these rabbis considered it almost fruitless to protest against this custom that, from a traditional perspective, was a denigration of the deceased, a failure to honor him or her. The Conservative rabbis contented themselves with "discouraging" the practice and limiting its public nature.

Reform sources suggest a change in American Jewish custom. In 1952, in the second volume of his *Reform Jewish Practice and its Rabbinic Background*, Solomon Freehof writes, "Frequently before the funeral the body of the deceased will 'lie in state' in an open coffin either at the home of the deceased or at the funeral parlor." He proceeds there to note the Orthodox objections and to dismiss them as based on superstition or derived merely from the prohibition against imitating Gentile custom.[31] In a responsum first written in 1958 but not published until 1977 Freehof describes this "lying in state" as a custom borrowed from non-Jews, and he "discourages as much as possible" the gentile practice of photographing the dead.[32] In August 1979, though, Walter Jacob indicates in response to a query the propriety of open caskets before the funeral service, that "in most cities, the casket … remains closed during the time before the service. Visiting before the service has been discouraged."[33] We see here evidence for a clear shift in Reform practice from a virtual endorsement to a clear discouragement of a central element of the American funeral.

ANINUT AND VISITATION BEFORE THE FUNERAL

With or without an open casket (or the presence of the deceased at all), visitation before the funeral is another area where American and Jewish expectations came into conflict. In Christian circles today, the funeral marks the end of official mourning.[34] The liturgy celebrates the resurrection of the deceased and his or her reunion with Christ. The Catholic liturgical reforms of the last decades reinforced this by calling for white vestments, not the traditional black for funerals. Therefore, it makes sense for the community to comfort the mourning family before the funeral itself. Today, this commonly takes place at the funeral home on the day or days preceding the funeral.

Traditionally, Jews buried as soon as possible, ideally on the day of death itself. This too falls into the category of "honoring the dead," as for the body to remain in the midst of a human society in which it cannot participate is considered a denigration of the personhood (or soul) still associated with it. Delay of the funeral was permitted only in order to obtain shrouds and a coffin. Today, a short wait for close family to arrive is also common.[35] During the period before the funeral, those close relatives required to mourn for the deceased are in a special status called *aninut* in which they may only prepare for the funeral. Because their focus is not properly on their own needs, it is considered inappropriate to comfort them or offer them condolences at this time. The community's obligations to *nihum avelim,* "comforting the mourners" begins only with the conclusion of the funeral as the mourners leave the grave and head home. Thus, visitation before the funeral directly conflicts with the ideational sequence of Jewish tradition. Where *aninut* lasted only a few hours or a day, this system worked well. Delay of funerals beyond this, as is common in the American funeral, creates a situation where it is virtually impossible not to offer comfort to the mourners.

Thus, in many parts of America, it became quite common for families to receive condolences, especially at the site of the funeral, for an hour or two before the funeral itself, and sometimes even the night before.[36] References in Freehof's responsa suggest that this custom was still in the process of emerging in the 1970s. Sources available to me currently do not include enough data to know whether this was a replacement for visitations with open casket the night(s) before, or something unrelated. Freehof's responsum on this matter, published in 1980, suggests that the custom may be a result of more and more people living in apartments who do not have room for large numbers of visitors.[37] Scattered family that gathers only for the funeral itself also contributes to the need to offer condolences before the ceremony. He suggests, "Since this new practice is a result of an unchangeable social situation, it would be almost hopeless to try to stop it. Thus it might perhaps be wise to follow the rabbinical dictum not to make a decision when we know beforehand that it will not be obeyed." It is better that people fulfill the *mitzvah* of consoling the bereaved at the wrong time than that they omit it altogether.[38]

Conservative rabbis do not deal directly with this issue, perhaps because their communities were more successful in maintaining the *shiva*, the week of mourning after the funeral. However, the recurrent discouragements of viewing the deceased and the added warning that no one should touch the deceased after the *taharah*, suggest that the context was of concern. Anecdotal evidence suggests that visitations before the funeral among Conservative Jews are not unknown. Greenwald, in his introduction critiquing the American funeral, sneers at those who leave their beloved alone at the embalmer's (i.e., the funeral home) without the traditional "watchers," coming only so that their friends and relatives can express their grief before running to where they are awaited for their game of dice.[39] Lamm, while also calling on the tradition of comforting only after the burial, goes out of his way to indicate that visiting at the funeral parlor the night before the funeral is imitation of the Christian "wake" and not simply American custom.[40]

The Conservative rabbis' warning that "[t]he traditional objection to touching the body after *Taharah* is always to be maintained"[41] may well reflect another non-Jewish custom, that of giving a farewell kiss to the body. This issue is of sufficient relevance that Greenwald gives it its own paragraph, citing the *Sefer Hasidim*.[42]

The Reform responsa on viewing cited above also draw on this medieval Ashkenazi source.

FLOWERS

The traditions of modesty and equality characteristic of Jewish funerary *halakhah* also fly in the face of the traditions of display of the American funeral.[43] Should Jewish funerals include flowers? Greenwald also received a query from Eliezer Werfel in Birmingham of how to handle these gifts, sent by friends and acquaintances of the deceased; should he not permit them to be placed on the casket, as this is a gentile custom? Greenwald suggests that no action should be taken unless it can be done without creating quarrels, which would themselves be inappropriate for a funeral. He also points to traditions of perfuming or incensing the deceased to counter the odors of decay and suggests that there is no real prohibition of aromatic plants or flowers. He concludes, however, with a reminder that Jewish funerals should not distinguish between rich and poor.[44] Freehof presumes that flowers will be placed around the coffin. He justifies this, saying, "it is not necessarily a Christian custom. Christian funerals were once as bare and unadorned as Jewish funerals were. The same modern aesthetic spirit which beautified Christian funerals has brought the comfort of flowers to Jewish funerals also."[45] In 1980, while discussing this ideal of equality in death, he comments "... therefore, it is virtually impossible to abolish or restrict the use of flowers, which the family and friends use to express their reverence for the dead ... ."[46]

Contrast these laissez-faire attitudes with that of the Conservative rabbis who declare in 1946, "The use of flowers at a funeral, being a Gentile custom, should not be countenanced under any circumstances." In 1961 they again voice that the Committee "strongly discourages th[e] practice" of using flowers in a synagogue funeral service.[47] It is unfortunate that these early *Proceedings* are so cryptic and record little of the discussions underlying the decisions. They apparently felt none of the need to respond to the emotional needs of those sending the flowers voiced by Greenwald and Werfel. We should also recognize that for most of human history, flowers were simply unavailable out of season. The masses of blooms available through florists today are very much a product of modern means of transportation and preservation. The use of flowers instead of black draperies and crepe ribbons is itself a product of the removal of visible mourning from the American funeral.[48] Thus, there is little deep precedent for expecting flowers at funerals. Received custom, that which determines the traditional responses here, was the product of a lack of technology as much as of principle.

CASKETS

In her scathing critique of the funeral industry, Jessica Mitford lambastes not only the funeral directors but also the florists in having a vested stake in ensuring that their clients spend as much as possible on a lavish funeral that will impress their family and friends.[49] We have already touched on embalming and burial clothes; what remains is the casket itself. This became a particular source of criticism of the funeral industry, not only because it can be the single most expensive item required for a funeral, but also because funeral directors, until it became illegal, gave a single price for the entire funeral package based on the coffin chosen. They employed techniques of display and sale in order to direct a bereaved family to the most expensive casket possible.[50]

Given this, we find surprisingly little discussion of appropriate coffins in the American Jewish literature. Jewish tradition, in its call for modesty and equality in death, prefers burial just in shrouds, or, if necessary, in a plain pine/wooden box. Greenwald has almost no discussion of this, except to note that he knows no source for the custom of prohibiting the use of any metal on this wooden coffin.[51] Lamm includes a more elaborate discussion, insisting, though, that the "type of casket purchased should not be determined by cost, and one should not worry excessively about how visitors will consider it."[52] The Conservative rabbis do call in 1938 for "observance of the regulations concerning a simple coffin"[53] but give no additional discussion in their halakhic proceedings. Freehof's *Reform Jewish Practice* addresses the issue in 1952, allowing any kind of complete casket, whether wood or metal. He finds precedents for burial of Jews in materials more durable than wood and argues that ultimately, even metal degrades.[54] His subsequent responsum, published in 1980, rejects any need for simplicity in the casket itself. He notes that even the Orthodox members of the Chaplaincy Commission allow decorating veteran's graves with flowers to honor them. He continues,

> If, therefore, it is virtually impossible to abolish or restrict the use of flowers, which the family and friends use to express their reverence for the dead, then by the same token, one cannot in a modern congregation properly prohibit any family from buying the most beautiful casket which they feel is in honor of their dead.

How then, does one fulfill the requirement of simplicity and equality? This, according to Freehof, applies only to items that are both durable and remain visible, like tombstones.[55] Given that he here extrapolates from an extraordinary use of flowers on existing graves to flowers at a funeral, and then to the casket itself, Freehof's logic can be questioned. His motivation is to find a way to validate halakhically what had become Reform *minhag*. Note, however, the contemporary Reform guidelines list "a simple kosher casket (a plain pine box)" in its example of a funeral plan.[56]

MUSIC

As we noted initially, many of these challenges to Jewish tradition are fundamentally aesthetic. Another area in which traditional Jewish funerals differed enormously from those of their Christian neighbors was in their openness to the use of music. Rabbinic tradition associates music with joy, prohibiting live performances during periods of personal mourning for a relative or periods of communal mourning like the three weeks preceding the Ninth of Av or the period of the Omer between Passover and Shavuot. Instrumental music is considered virtually necessary for expressing the joy of weddings, to the point that some communities hired gentile musicians to play for wedding festivities on the Sabbath, a day when, in the absence of the Temple (causing a perpetual state of mourning), musical instruments are forbidden. The Reform movement has largely chosen not to observe these traditional periods of mourning and their restrictions. Hence, its members and leaders do not associate lack of music with mourning. Mood-setting organ music is common at Reform funerals, and there is no limitation on adding other appropriate music to the funeral. In the Orthodox world, the opposite association holds, and music at a funeral, instrumental or vocal (as opposed to chanted prayers or psalms), would feel incongruous and even a transgression of the laws of mourning.

It is not surprising, then, that the Conservative rabbis find themselves straddling the middle. In 1935, the Committee on Jewish Law was asked whether it was appropriate for a cemetery to pipe in music for the entertainment of those visiting. They responded "that while Jewish law does not definitely prohibit such an innovation, it runs counter to Jewish sentiment and should not be in[t]roduced."[57] In 1938, in their minimum requirements for funerals, they ruled "music at the funeral should be prohibited."[58] Two years later, they recorded a more detailed response that took into account the Mishnah's description of flutes accompanying the *tannaitic* funerals. They note, however, that there are no accounts of this tradition's continuing. Hence, "[w]hile its practice would not be in contravention of Jewish law, it does run counter to Jewish sentiment as is evidenced by the fact that the custom fell into desuetude more than a millennium ago, and accordingly music at funerals should be discouraged."[59] The 1961 Proceedings indicate that the committee found itself without time to address the question of whether organs may be used at funerals.[60] Thus, at least for the period represented here, Conservative laity presumably regularly requested music at funerals. Their instinctual reluctance to include music may have been lessened not only by American models, but also by the movement's permission to synagogues to include organ/instrumental music on the Sabbath.[61]

FUNERAL IN THE SYNAGOGUE

Traditional *halakhah* does not decree any particular location for the funeral. The Mishnah's discussion clearly presupposes preparing the body at home following which various mourning rituals, including eulogies, accompany the procession to the cemetery. The most significant limitation on location is that death is a source of ritual impurity with which *kohanim*, people of priestly descent, may have contact only for close relatives or a *met mitzvah*, a person whom no one else is available to bury. This encouraged the development of dedicated buildings for the *hevra kadisha* and a restriction on the use of public buildings, like synagogues and educational institutions, for funerals. Orthodox tradition is that only the funerals of significant Torah scholars or outstanding righteous people take place in synagogues. Hence, Greenwald objects strenuously to the American custom of allowing any funeral to take place in the synagogue, even for people who have publicly flaunted fundamental halakhic norms and who thus are not Jewish role models. He suggests that these funerals mostly enrich the coffers of the synagogue. [62] In the 1951 addendum to this book, he rejects the suggestion that one use the lobby of the synagogue instead, for the entire building shares the holiness of the synagogue, and "lazy people and chatterers" use it as a prayer space.[63]

Before examining the Conservative and Reform responsa, we need to ask why people would prefer a synagogue funeral. Is this part of the "American funeral"? The literature on that phenomenon focuses on the funeral home and its or the cemetery's chapel, claiming that American funerals moved from the private home to the funeral home. It ignores almost entirely the Christian models of church funerals which dominate, at least today, for Catholics and many mainline Protestant churches.[64] Church funerals made logistical sense when burial was in the churchyard, but for many Christians, funerals belong in the sacramental context of a mass and hence in the church for its own sake. This suggests that locating the funeral in the church or synagogue is not particularly part of the model of the "American funeral." Another possible explanation for the preference for synagogue funerals is that the synagogue takes on the communal functions formerly performed by the *hevra kadisha.* Without a dedicated building for funerals, the funeral moved to the other Jewishly dedicated building. Ultimately, though, the answer is unclear.

This issue arises throughout the periods covered in this survey. In the Reform world, Rabbi Henry Berkowitz responds in 1923 to a congregation considering allowing funerals in the synagogue. He states that current practice is that the synagogue's rabbi and officials, and not simply the bereaved family, decide whether a particular funeral may be held at the Temple. This allows a control on the use of the Temple for ineligible funerals (he mentions as examples Christian wives and suicides). Fundamentally, though, a funeral is not less a religious service than a marriage, so the Temple is a legitimate space for it. He goes on to comment that because such funerals were historically only for people of special merit or distinction, a family's request for a funeral at the Temple is itself ostentatious. Iin the New York situation, however, where private homes are rarely large enough to accommodate a funeral, he recommends that all be eligible to use the Temple facilities, thus bringing the general principle of equality in death to this element of the ritual too.[65] Freehof's responsum, published in 1977, indicates that the custom of restricting use of the synagogue still holds, but that his congregation, Rodef Shalom, and others of comparable size had built chapels within the synagogue complex that were available to any member who requested them. This allows a liberalization of the tradition without specifically contradicting it .[66] In 1980, he emends this report somewhat, writing:

> My own congregation, even though the law was known that only scholars and leaders of the community should be eulogized or their funeral conducted from the main sanctuary, nevertheless decided that any member whose family so desires shall be buried from the main sanctuary of the temple. While this is not in accordance with the strict letter of the law[67] it is in harmony with the general tendency of equality in Jewish law.[68]

There is not uniformity on this issue in today's Reform world. The Union for Reform Judaism's guidelines emphasize that a congregation should have an explicit policy on who is eligible for a funeral in the temple itself.[69]

The question was even more persistent in the Conservative world. The Committee on Jewish Law responded to a query in 1935, writing that "it is doubtful whether the indiscriminate use of the synagogue for such purposes, even though it may open new sources of revenue for the congregation should be permitted."[70] In 1937, it ruled that it could not make global decisions as to who had sufficient stature for a synagogue funeral and that the local rabbi needed to determine this.[71] In 1947 they report that their policy is to discourage this as much as possible and "merely to acquiesce in the case of a man outstanding for his learning or piety."[72] In 1954, the majority reiterates this policy, but a minority, "of the opinion that it would be indelicate to draw such distinctions," calls for opening access to the space to any member who so requests.[73] In 1961, the issuesarises again but receives no answer.[74] Finally, in 1983, Rabbi Ben Zion Bokser concedes that in a case where a funeral in the synagogue is the only way to enforce Jewish practice (in the absence of a suitable Jewish funeral home), encouraging synagogue funerals is preferable, though he suggests bringing the casket only as far as the lobby, if possible.[75] This responsum needs to be situated within the growing movement to encourage and even enforce Jewish funeral practices in the American Conservative world. This larger concern, especially when reinforced by the calls for equality (a Jewish but also very American value), trumps traditional restrictions.

AT THE CEMETERY ITSELF

Where and how is the body buried?[76] Just as the American funeral embalmed, dressed, and made up the corpse so that it looked asleep rather than dead, so too it minimized contact with the realities of the grave. Gravesites were beautified, with artificial grass mats covering the bare earth, with the excavated dirt often temporarily carted away for the duration of the funeral. Simple machines for lowering the coffin allowed it to descend only a bit, level with the ground and covered with a grass mat during the interment ceremony, avoiding mourner's contact with the messy reality of the grave's depth and the finality of the actual burial. [77] Concrete vaults not only prevented the grave from subsiding with time, but sometimes also meant that the hermetically sealed coffin had no contact with the dirt and its bugs and worms. Alternatively, one could inter the body in a family or communal above-ground mausoleum, also avoiding the dirt and bugs. This distancing of the harsh realities of death was all deemed psychologically sound by the funeral industry, but presented halakhic challenges to Jews who deemed decomposition of the body and its return to its natural elements to be part of God's plan, and who defined the beginning of official *avelut*, mourning, as occurring with the filling of the grave.

Discussion of this new American model is not widespread. Greenwald, in his satirical introduction, criticizes failure to fill in the grave completely on the grounds that *aninut* ends only at this point, and reciting kaddish before then is improper. His screed also suggests that he is witnessing this among people who consider themselves "modern orthodox."[78] Lamm insists on burial in the earth, and indicates that to leave the casket at ground level and leave without completing the burial "is a distinct affront to the dead." He also speaks of the psychological benefit of hearing the thud of the earth filling the grave and of participating in this labor.[79]

In contrast, Freehof in 1952 describes as frequently the Reform practice, "in order to spare the feelings of the mourning family, to have them turn from the grave and return to their homes when the prayers are concluded but before the grave is filled." His explanation begins, "At first judgment it would seem to be against traditional Jewish law for the mourners to leave before the grave is filled." But after acknowledging that mourning cannot begin until this point, he points to an alternative medieval ruling that mourning may begin once the coffin is closed and the coffin is moved out of the house. This dispute derives from a disagreement over how, in the medieval French context of burials in the earth, to apply the tannaitic term for sealing the burial cave. Freehof uses this disagreement to justify leaving before the grave is filled, as long as one has the intention that the grave will be filled.[80] He later revisits this argument in response to a query about a funeral where the coffin was put in the grave but so late in the day that the gravediggers had stopped work. Under such unusual circumstances, mourning may also begin without filling the grave.[81] In 1989, Walter Jacob reiterates adherence to this custom, saying "As you quite properly state it is not our custom to fill the grave at all while the mourners are present, as this is especially difficult for them and at least in our present mood does not help them recover from their grief." As his subsequent discussion makes clear, this also enables the cemetery workers to use mechanical equipment to fill in the grave quickly. He does recommend throwing some dirt on the coffin, though.[82] The 2001/2005 Union of Reform Judaism guidelines include filling the grave as one of the traditional customs that some Reform Jews have reaccessed.[83]

Mausoleum interment involves no dirt at all. In large, communal, or family mausoleums, the casket simply slides into an individual, sealed vault. Freehof, in 1947, already accepts this form of interment, arguing that this actually corresponds better to modes of Jewish burial in caves and catacombs in biblical and rabbinic times in Palestine.[84] As he points out in *Reform Responsa* in 1960, while the cost of private mausoleums made them relatively rare, communal mausoleums are increasingly common, especially in the west, making this sort of interment a viable choice for many. He suggests that just as burial in closed coffins gradually became acceptable among "tradition-minded Jews," so too mausoleum burial may come to be accepted as a better analogy to biblical models than earth burial.[85]

The issue of mausoleums arises relatively late in the Orthodox community, at least as it is represented by Greenwald. He addresses the idea only in a footnote to the index of his book, indicating that this does not constitute burial and as such is forbidden.[86] In the 1951 addendum, called Volume Two of his book, he indicates that he was first asked about the propriety of mausoleum interments just as the first volume was at the printer. Fundamentally, burial must be in the earth. His discussion points out that "rich and assimilationist" Jews sought permission from Reform rabbis, who found sources for this in a number of medieval discussions about "built graves."[87] Tthey did not recognize, however, that in rabbinic times, these buildings were used to speed up the decomposition of the flesh, and afterwards, the bones were collected and buried in ancestral graves.[88] He adds, it also is forbidden to allow special conditions for the rich or to imitate gentile customs. However, Greenwald concludes this discussion, which was about burial vaults as well, saying:

But what good will all these words do us if we have no one to speak to? This is what the orphans[89] want and the embalmers who sell the vault have deceived them. If the *hevra kadisha* were to refuse to bury [the deceased] or if they were to tell them that they have an obligation to fulfill the verse "for you are dust and to dust you shall return,"[90] they will walk away and go to the Reform cemeteries where all is accepted.[91]

Insofar as Freehof's tradition-minded Jews are Conservative rabbis, Freehof would seem to be correct. In 1940, after remarking that the burials in Palestine were all in caves, i.e., in the ground, the Committee on Jewish Law records about mausoleums, "Whatever be the motive for the increasing popularity of this custom, strong attempts should be made to dissuade Jewish people from it."[92] In 1954, the Committee records that there should be no interment service in a mausoleum.[93] In 1961, the opposition is already muted. In response to a query whether mausoleums may be erected in Jewish cemeteries, the committee responds that the archives yield a mixed opinion: mausoleums cannot be outlawed, but they dissuade their use.[94] In 1964, a slightly fuller response advises that

such burial is not in keeping with Jewish tradition which asks for interment, and which is offended by ostentation. But the committee advised the rabbi not to carry his objections to the point of refusing to officiate at the funeral service.... It advised the rabbi to register his objection by refusing to attend the commitment service.[95]

The issue does not arise again in this committee's reports until 1983 when Rabbi Morris Feldman's detailed paper "May a Mausoleum be used for Jewish Burial?" is unanimously adopted by the committee. Feldman first reviews the history of mausoleums, including the nature of the current trend toward large communal structures that make efficient use of dwindling cemetery space instead of the older ostentatious private buildings. He then observes that rabbis are indeed officiating at committal services in these new structures and rules:

> Although there does not seems to be any impediment in Jewish law to using a mausoleum for burial, it should not be encouraged. Indeed, it should be actively discouraged since it is an obvious change from methods universally accepted today and its general publicized approval may create confusion. While it should be discouraged, we must recognize that it is permitted and that a rabbi may therefore officiate at an interment in a mausoleum.[96]

An addendum by David Lincoln suggests placing some sort of earth in the coffin so that the burial will still be in contact with dirt.[97] Functionally, then, the Conservative rabbis had accepted the reality of mausoleum interments.

CONCLUSION

Rituals surrounding death, in general, tend to be a place of great conservatism. The potential implications of doing something wrong, in the eyes of God, in the eyes of the deceased, or in the eyes of one's living community are sufficiently serious that people tend to want to "get it right" and avoid experimentation. In spite of this, a series of technological and social changes radically transformed the American funeral in the late nineteenth and twentieth centuries into something that, with slight alterations, bridged most ethnic communities and was distinctly American. Because Jews wanted and want to be fully American, they too accepted many of the values and ritual acts that constituted the American funeral. This generated a tension with the traditional halakhic requirements surrounding death.

For most of the twentieth century, these American values created the context for funerals in which Jews could make social statements of their Americanness. From the 1960's on, however, challenges to the by then established funeral industry created openings for the reassertion of an alternative set of values, the values of the traditional Jewish funeral. Over subsequent decades, traditional elements became more common in American Jewish funerals, not necessarily because they were halakhic, but because they express positive values, even American values like equality, lack of ostentation, and showing honor to the deceased.

The hypothetical lawyer, with whom we began, might today belong to a non-Orthodox synagogue with its own *hevra kadisha* in which his best (Jewish) friend serves. Because even the Orthodox funeral has been Americanized, there would be no embarrassing "old-world" mumbles; he himself might be offering a eulogy. The rabbi might be sensitive to the presence of our lawyer's non-Jewish colleagues and offer explanations of the various Jewish customs. His friends might happily risk the dry cleaning bill and help to fill the grave. Members of the lawyer's synagogue would also attend the subsequent *shiva*, perhaps not held for the full seven days, and their presence would make it easier for his colleagues to attend without discomfort. In other words, the processes of rebellion against the establishment in the 1960s, and the search for roots, ethnicity, and spirituality in subsequent decades have diversified the "American funeral" and allowed the American Jewish community to enter a process of negotiation away from its objectionable aspects and, incidentally, towards a greater compliance with traditional *halakhah*.

Notes

1.   As opposed to the immigrant generations that often maintained traditions around death even when they otherwise secularized. *Landsmanshaften* (societies of immigrants from the same European community), however secular, helped their members maintain distinctively Jewish funerary and mourning customs. See Daniel

Soyer, *Jewish Immigrant Associations and American Identity in New York, 1880–1939,* Cambridge, 1997, pp. 87– 91.

2. James J. Farrell, *Inventing the American Way of Death, 1830–1920,* Philadelphia, 1980, presents an excellent analysis of the emergence of these new approaches and rituals surrounding death. Gary Laderman, *Rest in Peace: A Cultural History of Death and the Funeral Home in Twentieth-Century America,* Oxford, 2003, continues the discussion, especially in light of the challenges to the "American Way of Death" that peaked in the 1960s. Jenna Weissman Joselit, *The Wonders of America: Reinventing Jewish Culture, 1880–1950,* New York, 1994, in her final chapter, "A Last Farewell," presents a portrait of American Jewish customs of burial and mourning up to the inception of the current return to tradition. See also Arnold M. Goodman, *A Plain Pine Box: A Return to Simple Jewish Funerals and Eternal Traditions,* New York, 1981, pp. xiiixvi. The book itself describes the ground-breaking model established by his Conservative Minneapolis congregation in setting up its own burial society according to Jewish halakhic practices, beginning in 1976.

3. For a discussion of Jewish funeral rituals, see my "Jewish Fuernarls: A Ritual
3. For a discussion of Jewish funeral rituals, see my "Jewish Funerals: A Ritual Description," *Proceedings of the North American Academy of Liturgy* (2001), pp. 108–122 (available with corrections at http://www2.bc.edu/~langerr/Publications/jewish_funerals.htm).

4. Samuel Dresner's critique, "The Scandal of the Jewish Funeral," Chapter Two in his *The Jew in American Life,* was published in 1963, the same year as Jessica Mitford's devastating critique *The American Way of Death,* New York, 1963, that caught the public imagination. Dresner's chapter is available at http://www.jewish-funerals.org/dresner.htm as part of a site titled *Jewish Funerals, Burial and Mourning* published by Kavod v'Nichum and the Jewish Funeral Practices Committee of Greater Washington (accessed August 24, 2006).

5. A centralized presence was established on the internet in 2000, *Jewish Funerals, Burial and Mourning* http://www.jewish-funerals.org/, with rich resources, information about the currently annual *Chevra Kadisha* conference, and links to *Kavod V'Nichum* (founded in 1998) that provides active support to those wishing to institute a chevra kadisha in their community. For contemporary Reform practice, see *To Everything There is a Season: Congregational Funeral and Cemetery Policies and Practices* (UAHC 2001; revised edition, URJ, 2005), available at http://urj.org/_kd/Items/actions.cfm?action=Show&item_id=7703&destination=

ShowItem. On p. 4, it notes that there have been dramatic changes in Reform practices in the last twenty years, on the one hand in the return to consideration of traditional practices, and on the other hand in the incidence of intermarriage.

6. This includes those posted on the Central Conference of American Rabbis' webpage at http://cc6arnet.org/documentsandpositions/responsa/ (as of July 2006). These include recent responsa that are marked as "not yet published."

7.   *Proceedings of the Committee on Jewish Law and Standards of the Conservative Movement 1927–1970*, 3 vols., ed. David Golinkin, Jerusalem, 1997; *Responsa 1980–1990, The Committee on Jewish Law and Standards of the Conservative Movement*, ed. David J. Fine, New York, 2005. That *Responsa 1991–2000, The Committee on Jewish Law and Standards of the Conservative Movement*, ed. Kassel Abelson and David J. Fine, New York, 2002, does not contain material relevant to our discussion is further evidence for the shifting landscape of concern in recent decades. One important issue there, burial of and mourning for non-Jewish relatives is very much a reflection on the American reality, but not on the "American way of death" per se.

8. New York, 1947. All translations are mine. I did not locate any relevant discussions in the published responsa of Rabbi Moses Feinstein or other leading American Orthodox rabbis. These same sets of issues and conclusions arise also in books written for popular audiences like Maurice Lamm, *The Jewish Way in Death and Mourning,* New York, 1969; rev. ed, 1981.

9. Sylvie Anne Goldberg, *Crossing the Jabbok: Illness and Death in Ashkenazi Judaism in Sixteenth- through Nineteenth-Century Prague,* trans. Carol Cosman, Berkeley, 1996 (French original 1989), Ch. 4. See also Arthur A. Goren, "Traditional Institutions Transplanted: The Hevra Kadisha in Europe and in America," in *The Jews of North America,* ed. Moses Rischin, Detroit, 1987, pp. 62–78.

10.   Greenwald, p. 87 #3.

11.   As described by Mareleyn Schneider, *History of a Jewish Burial Society: An Examination of Secularization,* Lewiston, 1991, p. 123f.

12.   *Proceedings ... 1927-1970,* Vol. 1, pp. 95, 168.

13. "YD 353:3.1983 Statement on Funerals in the Synagogue," in *Responsa 1980-1990...*, pp. 617-618.

14. RJP I:127.

15. "Funeral Folklore," *Recent Reform Responsa*, Cincinnati, 1963, pp. 149-153 (henceforth RRR). Freehof enclosed this responsum in a letter to his brother Louis dated November 17, 1958 (Rodef Shalom Archives [BA71 FF2]). My gratitude to Martha Berg, archivist at Rodef Shalom for locating the original of this and other responsa.

16. Walter Jacob, "168. Linen Shrouds or a Garment?," *Questions and Reform Jew-sh Answers: New American Reform Responsa* (NARR), New York, 1992, pp. 278-279, http://data.ccarnet.org/cgi-bin/respdisp.pl?file=168&year=narr. The 2001/2005 URJ guidelines list *taharah* and *takhrikhin* as optional after including them in its first example of a funeral plan (*To Everything...*, pp. 7, 9.)

17. Greenwald, p. 89, #14.

18. P. 91–92, #1, citing the Bah to YD 362end. In n. 20 here, he identifies this as his response to the same Rabbi Eliezer Werfel in Birmingham. Lamm, pp. 7–8, simply insists on shrouds.

19. With the exception of the person killed in an accident where in order to prevent further disfigurement to the body, the clothes are not removed.

20. Greenwald, pp. 51–52, #19. He relies heavily on Yehoshua Baumel's *Emeq Halakhah* I: 48. The issue arises again in Menashe Klein's *Shut Mishneh Halakhot* 16:122 with reference to those drawing on the precedents of the apparent embalming of Jacob and Joseph in Egypt preparatory to their transport back to Canaan. He denies that these were embalmings of the sort known today. Lamm includes a rather lengthy discussion, including of situations where preservation of the corpse is permitted, though preferably not by embalming (pp. 12–15).

21. Walter Jacob, "104. Burial at Sea (November 1984)," *Contemporary American Reform Responsa* (CARR), New York, 1987, pp. 165–166 (http://data.ccarnet.org/cgi-bin/respdisp.pl?file=104&year=carr), mentions embalming as generally prohibited but preferable to preserve a body so that it can be buried in the earth. The Conservative Movement's Committee on Jewish Law and Standards complains in 1961 that embalming is one of the questions lying unanswered for lack of resources. (*Proceedings...*, I: 482.) An undated report by

David Shohet that was never debated or adopted raises embalming as a subsidiary issue in his discussion of post-mortem examinations for medical purposes. He primarily reviews the history of embalming and makes no ruling regarding routine practice. (*Proceedings...*, pp. 1385–1386) Much of this history reflects the rhetoric by which embalming was touted as a superior procedure by the American funeral industry. See Gary Laderman, *Rest in Peace: A Cultural History of Death and the Funeral Home in Twentieth-Century America,* Oxford, 2003, pp. 6–11.

22 . Joselit, p. 268; Laderman, pp. 155–158.

23. As described by Mitford, pp. 56–57. I located various relevant sites on the internet, but one needs a password, supplied only to funeral directors, in order to view the merchandise. Examples include the Vera-Lee Garment Company and Rita Barbara, Inc., which sells "tribute fashions," cut appropriately for a reclining, casket body.

24 Refrigeration facilities make embalming less necessary in cases of delayed burial.

25. B. Moed Qatan 27a.

26. B. Horayot 13b.

27. Greenwald, p. 36, #10. See also his introduction, p. 13.

28 Lamm, p. 34, in "Viewing the Remains – A New American Custom," 26–34, written with the aid of a psychiatrist, originally published in *Journal of Religion and Health* (April 1966).

29. *Proceedings*, p. 94.

30. *Proceedings*, pp. 468–469.

31. (RJP II) Cincinnati, 1952, pp. 94–95.

32. "35. Photographing the Dead," *Reform Responsa for our* Time (RRT), Cincinnati, 1977, pp. 169–171. Louis Freehof's letter raising this question and Solomon Freehof's answers to him (the last includes the responsum verbatim as it was later published) are dated September 17, 1958 [BA71 FF2] and September 20 and 25th, 1958 [BA71 FF1] (Rodef Shalom Archives – my thanks to archivist Martha Berg for this and other references). This was apparently a regular practice,

at least in some parts of the country, as part of the focus on creating a positive "memory image" of the deceased. See Laderman, p. 22f.

33. "91. Open Casket," *CARR*, pp. 151–152, http://data.ccarnet.org/cgi-bin/respdisp.pl?file=91&year=carr. My own family history also suggests this transition. I am told that in Pittsburgh in the late 1940s and 1950s, my great-grandparents Stella and Marcus Aaron "lay in state" in their home before their funerals with the casket open. However, in 1983, I recall that their son, my grandfather, Marcus L. Aaron, refused even to enter the room containing an open coffin when making a condolence call for a non-Jew. Stephen Arnold, in private correspondence, reports this practice of viewings in Cincinnati through the mid-1960's.

34. In contrast to earlier periods where mourners demonstrated their ongoing grief by wearing special clothing for extended periods, while desisting from participation in public entertainment. See Farrell, p. 180.

35. Greenwald, pp. 36–40 #11 discusses the complicated question of what constituted improper delay of burial. Note 9 discusses whether waiting for children or a spouse to arrive constitutes "honoring the dead" or not. See also his introduction, pp. 12–13, and Lamm, pp. 18–21.

36. An informal survey on the HUCAlum listserve suggests that today, visiting immediately before the funeral is very common, even occasionally in Conservative and Orthodox circles, everywhere except the west, parts of the western Midwest, Alabama and Texas. Only a few respondents made reference to formal visitations one or two nights before the funeral at the funeral home or the private home. Even fewer recalled open caskets at these visitations, in all but one case in the 1960s and 1970s. Goodman, *A Plain Pine Box...*, pp.23–24, indicates that visitation at the funeral home was the object of united and forceful rabbinic protest, and that this was "the one issue in which Jewish funeral directors have had to accede to rabbinic sentiment and control." It is not clear whether this applies only to Minneapolis or more broadly.

37. This explanation seems unlikely. Urban European Jews and Jews in cities like New York had long lived in apartments without moving elsewhere to receive condolences.

38 Citing B. Yevamot 65b. "32. Visiting the Bereaved," *New Reform Responsa* (NRR), Cincinnati, 1980, pp. 133–138. See also his reference to this custom in RRT, p. 136. There he indicates that this is increasingly common. Freehof's

reference to a shift in housing preferences may reflect his own move to a smaller apartment in this period (according to Walter Jacob in private conversation).

39. Greenwald, p. 12.

40. Lamm, p. 35.

41. *Proceedings...*, p. 469, from 1959.

42. P. 34, #5.

43. See the discussion of Arthur G. Goren, *The Politics and Public Culture of American Jews,* Bloomington, 1999, p. 58, describing the public yet secular funeral of Yiddish dramatist and political radical, Jacob Gordin in 1909, where mourners were requested to arrive with flowers. Note that Gordin was also embalmed and no traditional liturgy was used (p. 59). The funeral itself, during which the casket was opened– included performances of music from his and other's theatre productions (pp. 60–62). Contrast this to Goren's description of the Yiddish writer Sholem Aleichem's funeral in 1916 which, from a halakhic perspective, was traditional (pp. 67–71).

44. Pp. 59–60, #34. Compare Lamm, 18, who echoes many of Greenwald's points, adding that this is a Christian custom.

45 RJP I: 135–137.

46. "36. On Covering the Casket," NRR, pp. 155–156. Note that the URJ's 2001/2005 Guidelines list flowers as "optional" (p. 9).

47. *Proceedings,* pp. 168, 492.

48. Farrell, p. 177. Farrell points out that some understood the flowers to be symbols of resurrection, but their primary function was to create a cheerful environment.

49. p. 22 and the relevant chapters.

50. Farrell, pp. 170f.

51. Pp. 182–183, #15. Note that he directs his energy against those objecting to the use of any coffin.

52. P. 16. He also points to FDR's insistence on burial in a simple wood coffin and JFK's transfer from the bronze casket used to transport him back to Washington to a simple wooden one for his interment. These are models of values that American Jews should emulate! (17-18).

53. *Proceedings...*, p. 95.

54. Pp. 98-101.

55. "36. Covering the Casket," NRR, pp. 155-157. Freehof's own tombstone follows this call for public modesty (Rodef Shalom's Westview Cemetery).

56. URJ 2001/2005 Guidelines, p. 7, reiterated in other contexts on pp. 4, 8, 9. Note that the Chevra Kevod Hamet founded in 1976 at Adath Jeshurun congregation in Minneapolis decided to build its own simple coffins (Goodman, *A Plain Pine Box...*, pp. 6-7).

57, *Proceedings*, p. 83.

58. *Proceedings*, p. 95.

59. *Proceedings*, pp. 125-126.

60. *Proceedings*, p. 483.

61. *Proceedings*: forbidden provisionally in 1939, p. 107; 1940 report of the Committee declining to make an absolute decision, with the majority forbidding it and the minority allowing it, 122-124; in 1953 a majority decided that a Jew may play the organ in the synagogue for Sabbath or holiday services, 370; in 1958, the majority accepted the view of Rabbi Phillip Segal (pp. 1315-1327, see also the responses, pp. 1328-1335, all published in *Conservative Judaism* 17:3-4 [1963]) that playing an organ does not violate the Sabbath or constitute an imitation of Gentile practices (pp. 419-420); in 1959, the Committee voiced an opinion that organ music is halakhically permitted, though perhaps not advisable liturgically and certainly prohibited for social dancing in the synagogue complex on the Sabbath, (p. 467).

62. Pp. 99-100, #12. Lamm fundamentally just discourages the use of the synagogue (p. 37).

63. Pp. 35–37. He also intimates that this suggestion may be coming from the lay leaders of synagogues rather than the rabbis, and points specifically, not only to the specific question he received from Peekshill (more often spelled Peekskill) New York, but also a situation in Chicago where this had become the custom.

64. Based on consultation with Catholic and Episcopalian clergy and a survey of the death notices in the Boston Globe. Boston lacks a large Evangelical community and is thus not representative of greater Protestant America.

65. "88. Burial from the Temple, also with Reference to Burial of Suicides," ARR, pp. 299-300, http://data.ccarnet.org/cgi-bin/respdisp.pl?file=88&year=arr.

66. "19. Funerals from the Temple," RRT, pp. 95-99. One should also note that the smaller spaces are much more intimate and appropriate to funerals.

67. He references here RRT, 95ff.

68. "29. Post-Funeral Eulogy," NRR, pp. 120-121. It is likely, as Freehof was long retired when both these responsa were published, that one or both of these responsa were actually written substantially earlier. The chapel mentioned was built in 1938, early in Freehof's tenure in Pittsburgh. See Richard L. Rosenzweig, "Rodef Shalom – Physical Spaces," in *Pursuing Peace Across the Alleghenies:The Rodef Shalom Congregation, Pittsburgh, Pennsylvania, 1856–2005*, ed. Walter Jacob, Pittsburgh, 2005, pp. 121-122. However, a search among Freehof's papers in the Rodef Shalom Archives did not locate evidence for an earlier date for the responsum.

69. Pp. 11, 12-13.

70. *Proceedings...*, p. 83.

71. *Proceedings...*, p. 89.

72. *Proceedings...*, p. 195.

73. *Proceedings...*, pp. 372-373.

74. *Proceedings...*, p. 482.

75. "Statement on Funerals in the Synagogue," *Responsa 1980–90...*, pp. 617–618. His paper was accepted by a vote of 10–2.

76. Cremation should also receive discussion here, but will not as it really requires a separate article. In addition, the issue arose much more forcefully in Europe, beginning in the late 19th c. and with the development of efficient technologies for incineration. It catches on much more gradually in America itself, and once it is reasonably common and accessible, memories of Hitler's crematoria and his systematic annihilation of Jews and their memory reshapes Jewish responses. Thus, this is not precisely a question of the influence of America on Jews.

Another set of topics that occupy American rabbis at great lengths involves participation of Jews in municipal or commercially run cemeteries. How necessary is a specifically Jewish cemetery or section of a cemetery? How necessary is it that people own their own burial plots? In addition, the realities of American conversion and intermarriage raise hordes of additional questions of who may be buried in a Jewish cemetery, and whether, if a gentile (or someone whose conversion one does not accept) is buried in a Jewish cemetery, how does that affect its holiness and legitimacy for Jewish burial? What about gentile relatives of converts? These questions definitely arise from the American Jewish reality, but neither the questions nor the answers derive from a negotiation with the "American funeral." They deserve treatment, but not here.

77 See Goodman's description, *A Plain Pine Box...*, pp. 81-82; and Farrell's analysis, pp. 135–136.

78. P. 13. In his main text, this enters only as a footnote, p. 213 #12, and there he identifies his source as a colleague from Hartford who suggests that this is an imitation of Reform customs.

79. Pp. 64–65. See also 55-58.

80. RJP II, pp. 103–106.

81. "23. An Unfilled Grave," NRR , pp. 97–99. Freehof draws here on his earlier discussions of when mourning begins during a gravediggers' strike, in "36. Delayed Burial," *Reform Responsa* (RR), Cincinnati, 1960, pp. 150-154; see also "36. Burial on the Holiday after a Strike," *Contemporary Reform Responsa* (CoRR), Cincinnati, 1974, p. 164.

82. "178. Filing [sic] in the Grave in Hot Weather," NARR, pp. 289–290.

83. P. 4.

84. RJP I, 123–125. He also points to a single exception to the rabbinic insistence since then on burial in the dirt.

85. "38. Communal Mausoleums," pp. 158–160. Freehof refers to this responsum to Rabbi David Polish in Chicago in the postscript of a letter to his brother Louis, written on September 18, 1958 (Rodef Shalom Archives, [BA71 FF20]). The remainder of this responsum deals with the question of the necessity of a separate Jewish cemetery, a modern question, but one that arose also in the European context. See also "45. Crypts as Family Burial Places," *Modern Reform Responsa* (MRR), Cincinnati, 1971, pp. 254–259, where he reviews again the argument for mausoleums in the context of a discussion about disinterring a family member to this mausoleum. Disinterment is another question that received enormous attention in the 20th century American literature, perhaps because of mobility, both economic and geographical.

86. P. 411, n. 1 to *qevurah b'qarqa* (burial in the ground).

87. Is Greenwald pointing to Freehof here? The sources include a commentary printed with the Rosh, MQ 3:79, end, Rashi, Sanhedrin 47b, s.v. *b'qever binyan sh'bana-o l'ma-ale min haqarqa*, and the *Nimuqei Yosef* on the same passage. In RJP I, the only text Freehof had published to this point, he only mentions the Rashi text. "Built graves" is Freehof's translation.

88. Greenwald entirely misses Freehof's point, which was that these ancestral graves were themselves burial caves, more akin to a mausoleum than graves dug individually out of the earth. Archaeological evidence from Israel supports Freehof's point.

89. I.e., the children of the deceased.

90. Gen 3:19.

91. *Kol Bo al Avelut*, Vol. 2, Brooklyn, 1951, pp. 48–49.

92. *Proceedings...*, p. 126.

93. *Proceedings...*, p. 375, here specifically in the context of removal of the body from a temporary placement in a vault into a mausoleum.

94. Proceedings…, p. 492. Compare this to their "strongly discourag[ing]" the practice of flowers at a synagogue funeral service in this same document. Both of these rulings lack the firm "yes" or "no" found elsewhere in this document, but "dissuading" is less forceful than "strongly discouraging."

95. *Proceedings…*, p. 514. The report continues that their code of funeral practices has been distributed to the membership.

96. *Responsa, 1980--990…*, pp. 619–623.

97. *Responsa, 1980-1990…*, pp. 624–627. Lincoln only adds more sources to Feldman's discussion, including an extensive citation of Freehof.

THE RELIGIOUS DUTIES OF WOMEN AND THEIR PARTICIPATION IN RELIGIOUS SERVICES

Samuel Adler*

This essay is divided into two segments; the first provides a theoretical discussion while the second is practical. It is of overwhelming importance to demonstrate that Judaism considers and counts women as full adults. It goes far beyond the practical conclusions described in the second portion of this essay. For only when we have become conscious of this fact, will we completely appreciate the earnestness and zeal of the feminine half of our religious community.

This is of vital importance not only because of the numerous practical implications and conclusions which must be drawn from this discussion. As I have demonstrated in the second part of this essay. Although it has been the policy of this rabbinic assembly to remain far from theoretical discussions, it is incumbent upon this assembly to speak out against erroneous concepts and practices.

The second portion of this essay will describe the religious obligations, of women, recognize them and develop them further. This step has up to now only been a *diseratum* for all those truly religiously inclined, however, without giving it any practical expression. We believe that this rabbinic assemblage [the Frankfurt Rabbinic Conference of 1845] cannot fulfill its primary and most deserving purpose of invigorating religious life and feeling, without absolute commitment to this task through word, deed, and enthusiasm.

The concluding section of this essay deals with the complete inclusion of women as fully counted participants in all public religious services. That step is absolutely necessary. A discussion of this matter, even though not a pressing practical issue is essential. It is basic to the entire proposal and therefore cannot be conveniently escaped or postponed.

* This essay has been republished here with my translation of the German introduction; the Hebrew text is reproduced without translation When originally published by Samuel Adler (1809–1891) in 1847, it represented the first effort, of the Reform movement, along with that of Samuel Holdheim (1806–1860) to deal with the status of women in a fundamental manner. Numerous practical changes had been made earlier in education, marriage, divorce, and liturgy; however without presenting a theoretical foundation for them. Adler's essay and that of Holdheim have been largely overlooked in the modern discussions of the feminist struggle in Judaism.

We should note that Samuel Adler did not continue his effort to change the status of women upon arriving in North America where he assumed the pulpit of Temple Emanu-el in New York. There were ample opportunities to do so, especially at the Philadelphia Conference of 1869 which was organized by him and David Einhorn (1809–1879), who had similar views. Adler seems to have concluded that this colleagues were not ready for such a decision.

In the 1840s both Adler and Holdheim agreed that the status of women had to be altered but they disagreed on the basis for such a change Adler felt that traditional texts could be interpreted to support his views; Holdheim considered such interpretations to take unwarranted liberties with the traditional texts. He preferred to understand such changes as part of the natural adaptation of Judaism to new circumstances.   A halakhic basis according to Holdheim's view was neither necessary or possible.

Holdheim's   essay, which attacks Adler's methodology was published as a booklet (D*ie religiöse Stellung des weiblichen Geschlechtes im talmudischen Judenthum,* Schwerin, 1846, 79 pp.).   It deserves publication in an English translation, not only for its feminist stance, but also for its methodological approach.

Adler's Hebrew essay republished here, originally appeared as an appendix to the proceedings of the Frankfurt Rabbinic Conference held in 1845 (*Protokolle und Aktenstücke der zweiten Rabbiner Versammlung abgehalten in Frankfurt am Main,* Frankfurt a.M. , 1845, pp. 234 ff.). In it

Adler justified the changes in the status of women in Jewish religious life that he sought through a broad and clear resolution that he proposed to the Breslau meeting. The resolution was referred to a Commission which did not report then or to any subsequent meeting. As those presiding over the sessions of the Frankfurt Conference sought a unified approach to practical changes, they avoided debate on contentious issues, however they agreed to the publication of Adler's essay as an appendix to the published proceedings. For more on this see my essay in this volume.

כאשר נחקור על מעמד ומצב הנשים בישראל בעניני התורה
והמצות, האם שוים הן חובות הנשים — מלבד הדינים הנקשרים
בגוף האיש או האשה, אשר מכריחים ההבדל בטבעם — לחובות
האנשים, או נבדלים המה, ואם נבדלים, איך ובמה ההבדל? הנה
לא נמצא בכל חנ״ך מענה בתורה לשאלתנו, כי התורה חתומה
נתנה, לא באדה כל פנות וסעיפי מצותיה, וחמכה הרבה על המנהג
הנהוג, אז בזמן נתינת התורה מימי קדם ואשר נהיה עי״כ לחק בישרא'
וכמסחה בעבור כן דברים הנודעים ונגלים לכל קהל עדת ישראל,
כאשר ג״כ תחן יד במנהגים כאלה לדורות אחרונים השונים במנהגם.

א• ואולם המחקר והמובן והפשוט לא יניחו ספק כלל, כי
שחיקת התורה כזה הודאה היא, שבכלל המצות אין הבדל בין נשים
לאנשים, ולא רצתה התורה לפטור נשים מאיזה מצוה ולחייבן באחרות,
לא היתה שוחקה מזה, גם איזה מקומות בתורה מראים זה לעין כל
רואה, כמה, ככה (דברים ה' א') „ויקרא משה אל' כל י ש ר א ל כי
שמע ישראל את החקים ואת המשפטים בו' ולמדתם אותם" הנה
כלתי ספק בכלל כל ישראל גם נשים הנה וגם אותן צוה' לשמוע
המצות וללמד אחהן (שמות כ"ג יל"ד), נ"פ בשנה יראה כל זכורך
כו' מראה כאצבע, כי לולי מלח וכורך גם נשים היו בכלל' הצווי,
הוא גלוי פנים על כל מצוח שבהורה, שלא הוציאה כהן נשים, שגם
הנה בכלל וכבר הרגיש התלמוד (קרושין ל"ד ב'), כראיה זו ורחאה
בקנה ולא ראינו ולא שמענו בכל' ספרי הגביאים והבאים אחריהם
רמז דבר להבדיל בין איש לאשה בדברים הנוגעים לתורה ולמצוה
ורק המשנה היא היתה הראשונה בהוראה זו, להשמיענו תורה חרשה
אשר לא חירש הבת עם הבן בנחלה אביו שבשמים בשוה, ומנורי'
נחלתן יגרע, ושלשה מקומות הן, אשר הציעה לנו דבריה בזה• א'
(כרכוה פ"ג ס"ג) „נשים ועברים וקטנים פטורים מק"ש ומן התפילין,
וחייבין בהפלה „ובמזוזה ובבה"מ•" — ב' (קרושין פ"א ס"ז ומ'חא'

„כל מצוח הבן על האב אנשים חייבים ונשים פטורות, וכל מצות
האב על הבן אחד אנשים ואחד נשים חייבין, וכל מצות עשה שהו"ן
אנשים חייבין ונשים פטורות, וכל מ"ע שלא הו"ג אחד אנשים ואחד
נשים חייבין, וכל מצות ל"ח בין שהו"ג בין שלא הו"ג אחד אנשים
ואחד נשים חייבין חוץ מבל השחית ובל תקיף ובל תטמא למתים•—
(מ"ח) הסמ־כות והתנופה וההגשות והק־מיצות וההקטרות והמלינות
וההואות והקבל־רות נוהגין באנשים ולא בנשים חוץ ממנחת סוטה
ונזירה שהן מניפות•"

ג' (סוטה פ"ג מ"ר) „מכאן אומר בן עזאי חייב אדם ללמד את
בתו תורה כו' ר"א אומר כל המלמד בתו תורה כא'לו לומדה תפלות•"

    ב• הנה לפנינו הלכות עצומות בדברים העומרים ברומו של
עולם, חדשות הן בעינינו, ובכל זאת לא טרחה המשנה להביא אף
ראיה אחת קטנה לתת טעם לרבירידה מן הכתוב או מן השכל, רק
ר"א, אשר לא רצה שילמר אדם את בתו תורה וראה לנגדו טענת
בן עזאי היא ל־כרו אמר טעמו ונמוקו, כי לא יהי' למוד התורה
לתועלת הנשים• ואיך נשכיל זאת שקצרה המשנה במקום שהיה לה
להאריך ולבאר מוצא מקום להלכות חדשות כאלה? אין זה, חי אנכי,
כי אם שההלכות ה֗ל֗ה לא מלכו הציאן מסדר המשנה, ולא הרשות
הגיד כהן לבני דורי, רק נוסרות במנהגי ישראל מדורות הקרמונים,
ומסרר המשנה סדר והעריך הקבל־ה כאשר מצאה ולא טרח לתת
טעם כרבר שאין צריך חזוק, כי חקנת הקרמונים עשהה דברים אלו
הנאסרים במשנוה הנ"ל כבר לחק קבוע בישראל־, וסה גם שטעם
הקרמונים, אשר תקנו כן, נמצא על נקל־ במעט עין, כאשר נראה
להלאה• ואם הגמרא על המשניות הנ"ל שקלה וטרהה לערוך מערכת
הדרוש ולהוציא לפי הנראה אלה ההלכות מן הכתוב, אין ספק שכל
השקלא וטריא איננה רק למצוא אסמכתא מרה מן הכתוב ואיננה
עיקרת• הלא חראה בקרושין כ"ט ב' יליף שאין האשה חייכת
ללמוד תורה ושאינה חייכת ללמד את בנה תורה גם שניהם
מטלה ולמרתם וכדרך אל־ תקרי, ואיך זה? איפוא ראינו שמדרת
דרשה זו של קרי היא ממרוח שהתורה נדרשת בהן? לא כי"ג דר'
ישמעאל ולא בל"ב דר"א בנו של ר"י חנליני! הנה כרור שדרשה זו
אסמכתא בעלמא היא, ועיקר הטעם מכח הסברא שאמר ר"א
במשנה סוטה הנ"ל, כאלו מלמדה תפלות• ולכן כל מערכרת הררש
בקרושין מן ד' ל־ר ולהלאה, להוציא הלכה זו, דנשים פטורות
ממ"ע שהו"ג, מן הכתוב ע"י םדוח ההיקש, ג"כ שקלא וטריא
בעלמא היא למצוא אסמכתא מה, כי אם חעיין שם חמצא

שעיקר זה הדרוש סובב הולך על ההלכה שנשים פטורות מח"ה, וכל
עיקר זאת ההלכה, כאשר ראינו, חקנת הכמים או קבלת הקדמונים
מסכרת עצמם. ואילו לא כן, איך תבין לבן עזאי שחולק על סברת
ר"א ואמר חייב אדם ללמד את בתו הורה, מאין הוציא הוא שנשים
פטורות ממ"ע שהז"ג? או ההיינה לפי דעתו ג"כ חייבות כהן? לא
ראינו ולא שמענו כן; אבל הדבר כאשר דברתי, הדרוש אסמכתא
ועיקר הטעם סברא. ובזה סרה קושיא התוס' בקדושין שם ל"ד א'
ד"ה גברי כו' הגראה בהשקפה ראשונה עצומה מאד, כי שם בגמרא
הוציאו שנשים היבות במזוזה מדכתיב בה: למען ירבו ימיכם ואמרו
גברי בעי חיי נשי לא בעי חיי, בחמיה. ומקשו התוס' דהאי קרא
משום הלמוד בעצמו (שכת ל"נ), אל מצוה ולמדתם אותם את בניכם
הנאמר למעלה ג"כ, ועוד בר"ח כתוב בהדיא כי היא חייך, ונהייב
נשים ג"כ בת"ח מטעם גברי בעי כו' והרוץ התוס' שם דחוק ורחוק
ואינו מתקבל ע"ש. אבל לפי מה שברךנו אין זו קושיא, כי הטעם
שפטרו נשים מח"ת הוא סברת ר"א במשנת סוטה הנ"ל, ואם ישאל
השואל: גברי כו' נשי לא בעי חיי? אנן נענה בתריה: הן, אבל
פעולות ח"ת אצל נשים חלוקה מפעולתה אצל אנשים, כי אם תוסיף
חיים לאנשים, חסר חיים אצל נשים, כי הוא כאלו לומדה תפלות. —
ואם הבקש עוד סעד וסמוכין לדעתי זו, הנה חמצאם בדברי הרמב"ם
הוא הגדר אשר החזיק (עיין הקדמה לס' משנה חורה והקדמה
לפירוש המשניורה סדר זרעים ופ"ב מהל' ממרים הל' א', בשטח
החוספורת (סוכה ל"א א' ד"ה ור' יהודרה) נגד רוב הקדמונים —
כאשר אבאר אי"ה במקום אחר — שהרשות נתנה לדרוש מי"ג המדות
הלכות חדשות לא שערום אבותינו, ושהרברה מההלכות הנמצאורה
בש"ם כל עיקר וסמקורן לא שום קבלה מאבות, רק איזור דרוש מן
הדרשות, ואעפי"כ לא חשב פה דרשורה גמרות הנ"ל לעיקר, וחקק
בראש הל' ח"ת "נשים ועברים וקטנים פטורים מח"ת" וכפ' י"ב
מהל' עכו"ם הל' ג' "וכל מצוה שהיא מזמן לזמן ואינה חדירה נשים
פטורות הוץ כו'" בלתי הת טעם וראיה לדבר כאלו הלכות מסורורה
הן, ובפה מלא אסר בפירוש המשנה למשנח קדושין הנ"ל כה דברו:
"ואמנם מה שהנשים מחוייבות ממצוות עשה ומה שאינן מחוייבורה
ממה שמגיע אליהן אינו חלוי בכלל, ואמנם נמסרים על פה
והמה דברים שכאו בקבלה כו'"· ואף הרי"ף והרא"ש הציבו
מאמר המשנה "כל מ"ע שהז"ג נשים פטורות כו'" בלא טעם
וסברא, כלי ראיה ומופת, והשמיטו כל השקלא וטריא בגמרת קדושין
ל"ד הנ"ל המטרחת למצוא ראיה מן הדרוש אל זה הכלל, ורק דרשת

הגמרא ד' כ"ט כ' הנ"ל לפטור נשים מח"ה מקרא דולמדתם העתיקו,
כאשר נ"כ הרמב"ם בפירוש המשנה לסוטה פ"ג מ"ד החזיק בדרישה
זו וחשבוה לעיקר, ואדבר מזה מיד להלאה.

ג. נחקרה נא לדעת עומק כונת הקדמונים ז"ל מה ראו על
ככה ומה הגיע אליהם, לבנות חומה בצורה בין מצב הנשים לאנשים
בעניני ההוראה והמצוה, ולשלול מן הנשים רב טוב, באשר פטרו
אותן ממצוה ת"ה ומכל מ"ע שהז"נ זולת מעטוה? ואם יענה העונה,
הן זה בעבור כי היו הנשים בעיני הקדמונים דלות העם ופחותי הערך
ולא נחשבו להם ליקח חלק באלהי ישראל ובמצוותיו הנחמדות כאחד
איש ישראל, אנחנו נוסיף לשאול, א"כ איפוא מדוע פטרו אותן
ממ"ע שהז"נ דוקא ולא משאר מצוה עשה? אף גם העיקר מהאחר,
שהשוה הכתוב אשה לאיש לכל עונשין שבתורה, סותר השובה זו,
כי זה אמנם יתר בל המוט, לפי מדרגת נפש אדם וכח שכלו עונשו
על העברות, ורק בעבור זה קטן אינו בר עונשין, ואם תהינה הנשים
פטורות ממ"ע שהז"נ בעבור שפלה נפשוהן, מרת הצדק תבקש שגם
עונשן על עברוה ל"ה יהיה קל מכאנשים, והשופט כל הארץ לא
יעשה משפט!

טרם נחורה דעתנו בזה, נשים עין אל דברי הרמב"ם בפ"א
מהל' ה"ת להבין כונתו ולראות על מה אדניו הטבעו. בראש הפרק
שם כתב: "נשים ועברים וקטנים פטורים מח"ה, אבל קטן אביו חייב
ללמדו תורה שנאמר כו'" ושוב בהלכה י"ג שם כתב: "אשה שלמדה
יש לה שכר, אבל אינה כשכר האיש מפני שלא נצטוית כו' ואע"פי
שיש לה שכר צוו חכמים שלא ילמד אדם את בתו תורה מפני שרוב
הנשים אין דעתן מכוונת להתלמד, אלא הן מוציאות ד"ה לדברי
הבאי לפי עניות דעתן, אמרו חכמים כל המלמד את בתו תורה
כאלו למדה תפלוה". בשתי בחינות נפלאים דברי הרמב"ם אלה, חו
בזז תליא. א' איך הבין מחלוקת בן עזאי ור"א בסוטה הנ"ל אם חייב
אדם ללמד את בתו תורה או לא; ב' הכונרה שכיון במאמר ר"א
כאלו מלמדה תפלוה". מי שיש לו עין לראות יראה ויודה, שרעת
הרמב"ם דנשים פטורות מח"ה אליבא דכ"ע ואין מחלוקת בדבר, ורק
בן עזאי רצה שיחויב האב מדרבנן ללמד את בתו תורה, אע"פי שהיא
אינה מצוה על ח"ה מטעם שאמר. ומה שהכריח הרמב"ם להבין כן,
נראה בעיני, מפני שמצא בכל הש"ם לדבר מוסכם ומקובל שנשים
פטורות מח"ה בלתי שום ערעור ומחלוקק, ככה בסוטה כ"א א' מקשה
הגמרא: "זכות דמאי אילימא זכוה דתורה הא אינה מצוה ועשה",
ולא אמרה: הניחא לבן עזאי וכו' כרדכה בשאר מחלוקק; וכן בקדושין

ר' ל"ד הנ"ל יליף רנשים פטורות ממ"ע שה:ז"ג מתפילין ותפילין מח"ת,
מה ח"ת נשים פטורות אף כו' · ולא מקשה הניחא לר"א אלא לבן
עזאי וכו' · ואף דרש"ת הגטרא בקדושין כ"ט כ' הנ"ל דאשה אינה
מחוייבת ללמוד תורה וללמד ארת בנרה מקרא של ולמדרהם חשב
לעיקר, כאשר העירותי למעלה סוף אות ב', והיה קשה לו גמרא זו
אליבא דמאן? לבן עזאי נשים חייבורת בת"ה, ולר"א דפטורורת אין
הטעם מקרא דולמדתם, רק מסברא מלמדרה תפלות? ולכן חירץ
לעצמו, שנגמרא זו אליבא דכ"ע, וגם כן עזאי מודרה דנשים פטורות
מת"ח מדרשה זו של ולמדרחם, אבל אומרו: חייב אדם ללמד את בהו
תורה רצונו היב מדרבנן כנ"ל · ואע"פי שלפי דרך זו סוגייח נגמרוה
האלה ג"כ אליבא רבן עזאי, אפ"ה פסק הרמב"ם כר"א מכמה טעמים,
חדא שרבי יהושע במשנרה סוטרה הנ"ל שאמר: רוצה אשה בקב
ותפלות כו' נראה שהוסיף באור לדבירי ר"א ומסכים עמו, ועוד דכמה
מקומות בש"ם סחמן כר"א, בכתובורת מ"ט א' ובבבא קמא א' אמרו:
מצוה ליון ארת הכנרת ק"ו לבנים דעסקו רעסקו בחורה דבירי ר"מ,
ובכתוכוה ק"ח ב' איתא במשנה:' ובנכסים מועטים הבניה יזונו והבנים
יחזרו על הפתחים, ארמון אוכר בשביל שאני זכר הפסדחי"; ומקשה
הגמ' על דברי ארדמון: מאי קאמר? ומחרץ אביי "ה"ק בשביל שאני
זכר וראוי לעסוק בחורה הפסדחין, וכאבורה פ"ה, כ"א: אמר
יהודה בן חימא "בן ה' שנים למקרא כו' בן י"ג למצות, ומחוך דבריו
אלה האחרונים יוצא ברור שמדבר רק מאנשים לכד ושאף ראשירה
דבריו בן ה' שנים למקרא נמשכים רק אר"ל אנשים ולא דבר מנשים
כלל מאיזרה וזמן יחחילו ללמוד התורה, בלחי ספק בעבור שהן לפי
רעתו לא תלמדנה כלל התורה, וכמו כן בכתובורה נו"ן ע"א "האמר
אכיי אמרה לי אם בר שיח למקרא בר עשר למשנה בר חליסר
לחעניתא מע"לע וכבחנזקה כת חריסר' הנה קבעה הזמן כתנוכרת
רק לעניַן חעניַת ולא לעניַן לסוד מקרא ומשנה, וראי בעבור שאינם
נהוגים כלל בהנוקַב (ועיִי' רש"י שמד"ה ובחנוקַת וחוסף' ר"ה ובת הריִסָרן)· וכן
חמצא בנרה מ"ה ב' נחן ר"ש כררב יצחק טעם לדעה רשב"א שסכר חנוק ממהר
להחכחם יוחר מחנוקַתואמר: "מהוך שהתנוק מצוי בביה רבו נכנסח בו
ערמומיַת חחלה' א"כ ברור שהי' מנהג פשוט או בכנות שלא באו אל
בית הספר, וזה וראי מטעם ר"א כל המלסר כו' כאלו סלמרה תפלוח·
— ובדעה הרמב"ם הוו בכונת מחלוקַת ר"א ובן עזאי חלוי ג"כ פירוש
הרמב"ם כמאמר כאלו מלמרה תפלות, כי אם אמח הוא שרעה ר"א,
כאשר הבין הרמב"ם, שנשים לא ידעו ולא יכירו את ספר התורה,
והאב המתעסק להבינו אה כהן, נבלה עשה בישראל, הם סלהוכיר!

ודאי אין לנו סמוכ רק לבאר מאמר ר"א: כאלו מלמדה תפלות כאשר
כארו הרמב"ם, "שהנשים עניורה בדעתן ויוציאו דברי התורה לענינים
זרים וחולין, יהפכו מתוק למר וקדושה לטומאה ואחריהן ערי אובד•

ד• ואולם על שטח הרמב"ם קשה לי הרבה, חדא מאין ראה
או ידע כן שהנשים עניורה בדעתן מחק הטבע? ואדרבה בנדה ד'
מ"ה ב' סתמה המשנה :רבי, וכך ההלכה, שבאשרה נדריה נבדקין
וקיימין שנה אחת קודם מבאיש ונחן רב חסדא טעם לזה מפני
"שנתן הקב"ה בינה יתרה לאשה יותר מאיש", ואפילו רשב"א
דפליג שם וכו' שתינוק ממהר להתחכם טעמו מתוך שהתנוק מצוי כבית
רבו כו', אבל אם הנשים גם הן חלמרנה מקטנותן, אזי חמהרנה גם
הנה להתחכם ולא היו עניות בדעתן כלל וכלל• ואם מצינו שרשב"י
גזר אומר "נשים דעתן קלה עליהן "(שבת ל"נ כ'), הפרש גדול יש
בין קלות הדעת לעניות הרעת, ועד שאפילו קלות דעתן גם היא
איננה רק פרי חסר למודן ולא הראה ולא חמצא אם חחזקנה את
רוחן מקטנותן בתורה ובחכמה; ומזה הטעם בעצמו גם דרשה של רב
הונא (מנחות ק' א'), "חביאו בניך מרחוק אלו גליות שבבל שדעתן
מיושבת עליהן כבנים ובנותיך מקצה הארץ אלו גליות שבשאר ארצות
שאין ידרתן מיושבת עליהן כבנות" גם היא איננה שום סעד וסמך
לרעת הרמב"ם הלוו- שניח במשנה קדושין ד' פ"ב ע"א איתא: "ולא
חלמר אשה סופרים" ונתנו בגמרא שם טעם לוה, "משום אבהתא
דינוקי", והיה לה לגמרא לרחת טעם יותר מספיק מפני שאסור
לאשה לעסוק כלל בד"ח, שהרי אפילו הורה שכבהב לא הלמור
האשה לכתחלה לפי דברי הרטב"ם שם בסוף הפרק? של יש יח
בחגיגה ד' ג' א' דרש ראב"ע "הקהל אה העם האנשים והנשים והטף
אם אנשים באים ללמוד נשים באות לשמוע" ואמרו בירושלמי ע"ז
רוה דלא כבן עזאי דאמר חייב אדם ללמוד את בתו תורה (עי'
תוס' שם ד"ה נשים) ולפי סברת הרמב"ם מדין התורה נשים פטורות
מ"ח אליבא דכ"ע ורק מדרבנן אמר בן עזאי שיחוייב האב ללמדה
את בתו? רביעיה כבר העירותי למעלה כאות כ' שדרשה הגמרא
קדושין כ"ט ב' לפטור נשים מלמור ד"ח ומללמד את בנה הורה ממלות
ולמדתם ולמדחם אי אפשר כלל להיוה דרשה גמורה ועיקר הטעם
על כרחך הוא סברת ר"א דהוה כאלו למדרה הפלות, ואף דרשרת
הגמרא שם שאין האב חייב ללמד את בחו תורה סולמרתם אוחם
את בניכם ולא כנוהיכם א"א להיות דרשה גמורה, דכמה דוכתי
בקרא שכנוה בכלל בנים הן כמו: בנים אתם לה' אלהיכם (דברים
י"ד א'), שהוא השרש לכל הלאוין הנאמרים בפרשה זו,

וכדומה??*) ואף גם זאת שלפי שטח הרמב"ם אשה שלמדה תורה
אעפ"י שאינה מצווה יש לה שכר, ולטעמידה אזיל, כי הוא פירש
מלמדה תפלות "מוציאה ר"ה לדברי הבאי" ולכן ודאי אם למדה
ולא הוציאה לדברי הבאי שכרה אתה, ומרוע לא! אבל א"כ כשהקשה
הגמרא (סוטה כ"ט א') "זכות רמאי אילימא זכות דתורה הא אינה
מצווה ועושה" וטרחה. ויגעה הגמרא בזה הרבה עד של בסוף אמר
רבינא "לעולם זכות דתורה ורקאמרת אינה מצווה ועושה כו' באגרא
דמקרין בנייהו ונטרן להו לגברייהו כו' כי לא פלנן בהרייהו,
ולמה לא חירץ בפשוט מאד, שאע"פי שאיננה מצווה מ"מ יש לה
שכר וכמאמר הרמב"ם? — ולכן י"ל שאין הדין עם הרמב"ם, וכונת
ענין זה כך הוא. הרבר ידוע כמה גרלה מצוה זו בעיני הקדמונים
לשקור ולהגות בתורה ה' יומם ולילה, והיא מהדברים שאין להם
שעור למעלה, וכל הדברים שהפירורח נאכלים בעה"ז והקרן שמור
לעוה"ב ה"ח בראשם וכנגד כלם. אבל "אל הצדק הרבה" גכול
שגכלו ראשונים, והמה ראו גם ידעו שאם אף הנשים יהוקו במצוה
זו וימאסו בכל מלאכה לעסוק רק חמיד בלי מניעה בחורח ה', הנה
סדר הבית ישהה וגדול הבנים לא יהיה עוד והנהגת העולם יתטרד
ויבולבל, ופה יחאסת המאמר: אלסלא עליא לא מהקיימין איחכליא
(חולין צ"ב א'); ולכן כבר קרמוני הקרמונים התקינו והנהיגו ועשו חק
בישראל שנשים לא יכלו ימיהם בכהס"ד ופטורות הנה ממצוה הגדולה
הזאת. והגירה כו יומם ולילה. והרי זה רומרה ממש למרה שמצאנו
בחגיגה ה' ב': "ה"ר שלשה הקב"ה בוכה עליהן ככל יום על שאפשר
לעסוק בחורה ואינו עוסק וע"ל שאי אפשר לעסוק בחורה
ועוסק וכו'" ואם המשנה בקרושין הנ"ל גזרה אומר: כל מ"ע
שלהו"נ אחר אנשים ואחד נשים חייבים ולא זכיה רבר ממצות ח"ח, הטיב
ר' יוחנן שם (ל"ד ה') לומר "אין למדין מן הכללות אפילו במקום

---

*) ואף דרסת הגמרא בקדושין סס כ"ט א' שגסיס אינן בכלל מנות פדיין
הבן, ר"ל שאינן צריכות פדיין מדיוקא דקרא וכל בניך תפדה בניך ולא
בנותיך, נס היא איננה עיקרת, רק עיקר הטעם שנכות אינן בכלל פדיין
מהוראת הכתובים עגמס במדנר ג' ויתר מקומות בתורה המראים לעין כל
שרק זכריס יהיו קדוסים לה' וכמ"ש הסמ"ג נאר הטיב בעגין סי' קמ"ד ע"ש
ובוה נפלה מעצמה ג"כ תמיהת התוס' בקדושין ל"ז א' ד"ה הקנלות ע"ש
ולא אאריך.

שנאמר בהן חוק", ולא היה מעולם חכם מישראל חולק על התקנה
הגדולה הזאת אשר היא יסוד החיים וכל דרשות הגמרא להוציא
הלכה זו מן הכתוב אסמכתורה הן כנ"ל, ועיקרה סברא ישרה, וכן
מה שדרשה הגמרא בקדושין כ"ט כ' שאין האשה חייבת ללמד את
בנה תורה אסמכתא היא, כי הדרשה אינה מאחה המרות שהתורה
נדרשת בהן, וכונת הלכה זו לא שתגריל בנה בלתי תורה, חלילה!
רק שהיא בעצמה אינה מהוייבת לקח ספר וללמדו, כאשר היא
המצוה בעצם וראשונה אצל האב, כי זה גם כן אינו מתאים אל
מצב האשה ותובהה בהררכת הבית, ומופה הוזך לזה בב"כ כ"א א'
"בהחלה מי שיש לו אב מלמדה תורה, מי שאין לו אב לא היה
למד תורה, מאי דרוש ולמדתם אותם כו' (עיי' הוס' שם הגירסא
הישנה שנראה עיקרה) התקינו שיהו מושיבין מלמדי תנוקות כו'".
הנה לפנינו שרק מלמד הבנים בעצמם נפטרו הנשים, אבל אחר
תקנה יהושע בן גמלא שהיו מלמדי תנוקות בכל עיר ופלך, גם
הנשים מחוייבות לשלח בניהן שמה ולגדלים לתורה*). אמנם אם
הקרמונים לא רצו שיבלו הנשים את ימיהן בבית המדרש, לא טוב
היה בעיניהם בלרזי ספק ג"כ, שהנשים תגדלנה בלי דעת קונן וחפץ
צורן; מצוה ולמדתם אותם את בניכם על הבנות ג"כ נאמרה, ולפי
מאמרם ז"ל במשנח קדושין הנ"ל כל מ"ע שהו"ג וכל מצות ל"ת וכל

_____

*) וכמו כן ממם הכוונה באותו מאמר שם שאשה אינה מחוייבת למול
את בנה, לא שתגדיל אותו ערל, רק שהיא בעצמה אינה מחוייבת לקח
סכין ולהסיר ערלת בנה, כאשר היא המצוה תחלה על האב, והטעם נגלה
ונכבד, בעבור שהאם לבה רך, והתורה חסה עליה ולא תבקש להפך אותו
אכזרי. — ופירום זה בכל הדברים בעיני ברור, ואולי גם הפוסקים המביאים
ברייתא זו כצורתה הבינוה כך אבל נפלאתי וחיל ויגון אחזוני בראותי בס'
מנדול עוז להרב יעב"ץ תעלה ג' ד' מ"ג ע"א לבנים זרים וקנים,
לא יוכל לב אנוש הכילם, ח"ל: "לענין הפרשה מאסור כן ובת שוית לכל
דבר — נד"א נאב, אבל אמו אינה מצווה עליו" פה ראיתו עד
היכן מניעה הדרישה בדת בעינים סגורות והאמונה החלוטה המעולת
פקחים; דעתו של רב התובל הזה, אשר מרר ורב והלית אם הכעס
והבאגאה לתועלת הדת והתורה — לפי מחשבתו — במחנה ישראל, כי כל
הנשים בישראל לא יעשו עולה, אם תגדלנה בניהן לבנים זרים ומשחיתים,
התורה לא תהיה קדושה להם ואין אלהים כל מנימות!

אורך ורוחב דיני המוסר חובה על הנשים, ואיך יעלה א"כ על דעת
שום בר דעה שתגרלנה בלא הורה! אבל הדבר כאשר אמרתי, חיוב
ידיעת המצוה ככר נשרש במצוה עצמה ואין הבדל בה בין נשים
לאנשים ורק ממצוח והגית בו וכו' לבד פטרו הנשים ומטעם הנ"ל
כאמור. זה בלהי מחלוקת כלל. ואם חבקש עוד מופת לזה הנה
תראה בסנהדרין צ"ד ב' שם שכהו ארה דוקיהו שפזר תורה בדורו
ואמרו: "בדקו מדן ועד באר שבע כו' מגברת ועד אנטיפרס ולא
מצאו חנוק וחנוקה איש ואשה שלא היו בקיאין בהלכות טומאה
וטהרה." — ואולם אפן למה הבנות זהו מחלוקת בן עזאי ור"א.
בן עזאי אומר חייב אדם כו' וכונהו חייב ללמד את בהו כל ספר
החורה עם כל הבאור כמו לבנים אין הבדל ביניהם, רק אח"כ אם
יורעה ומכרת הכל לא העמוק בו רמיד, ור"א סבר שות מורה אי
אפשר להפרד, כי אם למדה ספר וירדה בעימק ענייני התורה כמו
הבנים, הלכך מזה רוחה ולנה, רעזוב עסקי הבית והעסוק רמיד
בתורה וזהו כונת דבריו: כאלו מלמדה תפלוה, שמונע אותה מלעשות
חובוחיה המוטלוח עליה בהנהגה הבית. ולא פירש לנו ר"א על איזה
אפן תלמדנה הנשים יראת השם ורצון קונן לפי דעתו, בעבור כי פשוט
הוא וכבר הי' ההרגל כן בימיהם בלחי ספק, שהראב יניד לבתו
הדינים הנצרכים לה, האמונה והמוסר בטעמם ונמוקם, רק שלא
קבעה מדרש ללמד ספר, מטעם הנ"ל. וסחמא רגמרא בקדושין כ"ט
ב' ויהר מקומות הנ"ל באמרך כר"א ולא כבן עזאי. — ואם חשוב
עהד. קורא נעים, לחזור על כל המקומות בש"ם המוקשים לפי שטה
הרסב"ם, חמצא לפי דברינו אלה הכל על ל נכון, רק לא אאריך
בזה עוד.

והיוצא לנו מזה להלכה ולמעשה הוא, שאין חפץ לה' בכסילים
ושגם נשים צריכוח ללמוד תורח ה' ורצונו עד שתהא שגורה בפיהן
וחרוחה על לוה לבן, ולא לבד ידיערת המצוח, רק באמה גם ספר
הורה ה', כי אם גם ר"א לא רצה שילמדו הנשים ספר, לומנו רבר,
אכן בזמננו שהנשים ילמדו ספרים חצונים הרבה, אשר ארם מחשבוה
הורות ורעיונות הנשחחוה טמון בקרבם, והם המלמדים אוחן חפלורה
ממש, מוטב שיהגו כדברי אל חי ויהיו להן סם חיים, מאשר ישעו
כרברי שקר, וכל מי שאינו מוכה כסנורים, יורה לזה.

ה. ומעחה נקל"ל לנו נ"כ ל'מצוא טעם נכון ומספיק לחקנורת
הקדמונים, לפטור נשים מרוב מ"ע שהו"ן, והכל סובב הולך על
קוטב זה הכלל שהנהנו, כי חובת הנשים בצרכי הבית לא יניחו אוהן
לעשוה שום מצוה הנקשרה בשעה מְגֻבֶלֶּח. וְהִנֵּה זֶה כָּמו וְהָן וְאכל

שפטרו אותם הקדמונים ג"כ לפי אומר דעתם הישרה סק"ש, והאכל
אפילו מכל מצוה האמורו בתורה, בעבור ששקלו במאזני צדק טרדות
הרבות של אלה האנשים והקילו ע"כ משא מצות המעשיות מעל
שכמם. (עי' רמב"ם פ"ד מהל' ק"ש ה'א) . וזה באמת מופת חורך
לחכמת הקדמונים מנבילי הדת בישראל, וראיה נפלאה מהחרות
הגדולה, אשר לקחו לעצמם לשלוט במצות המעשיות כפי רוחב דעתם
זהכרח עניני הזמן והעולם. וראיה ברורה לזה שרק מפני עול צרכי
הבית פטרו נשים מח"ת וממצות שהו"ג, לא בעבור חשבון פחיתות
הערך, הן הנה מצוה חלה והדלקת נר שבת, שהרי אע"פי שהדלקת
נר שבת מצוה שהו"ג היא העטיסוה הקדמונים על שכם הנשים בפרט,
אין זה כי אם בעבור שאלה המצות לא לבד לא יתנגדו לעסקי הבית,
רק גם יחאיסו סאאד לורד העסק, וכמ"ש כבר רש"י בשברה ל"ב א'
ורע"ב פ"ב דשבח"פ"' והרמכ"ם פ"ה מהל' שבת ה"ג . — ורק עפ"ז
מבואר איך יוכלו נשים לברך על מצוה שהו"ג אם ירצו לעשותן ולאמר
וצוונו כאשר שפטורות אפילו מדרבנן? והרבה טרחו בזה החוס' (ר"ת
ל"ג א' ד"ה ה"א) ולא מצאו טעם, אבל לפי הנ"ל ניחא כי מעיקר
הדין אין הבדל בין נשים לאנשים, רק חכמים פטרו אורן בעבור
טרדות עסקי הבית, ולכן אם אינן טרודורת ועושין המצוה, יוכלו
לברך ג"כ.

אחשוב עתה הדרכר הזה מבואר וסבורר די צרכו, ויצאו
רבורחינו הראשונים ז"ל סן הלענ והקלם, אשר גלילו הבוערים בעם
על ראשם אודורת דעתם ואוסרם מחוברות הנשים; יפה ביונו, יפה
הורו, אין פרץ ואין צוחה, רק הנהה והרוחה.

ו. ואחרי הדברים והאמת האלה נראה בעיני דשלא כדין
עשו הדורות האחרונים להוציא נשים מכל דבר שבקרושה ושלא לצרפן
לסניך עשרה, ואין שרש ואין רמז למנהג הזה במשנה ואין לו מקור
בש"ס, וסרסמא דרתלמודא מורה ההפוך, כי במגילה (כ"ג ב') חשב
במשנה כל הרברים הצריכים להיורת בעשרה ולא נזכר שם מידי
שאין נשים בכלל העשרה, והגמרא שם שהוציאה הלמוד דכל דבר
שבקרושה בעשרה מונקדשתי ברזון בני ישראל, אולי יאמר האומר:
פה נרמז שאין נשים בכלל, כי בני ישראל ולא בנורת ישראל? אבל
דיוק זה לא יחצן כלל וכלל, כי מלבד שכל הדיוקים הנמצאים כזרה
וכיוצא בזה אינן דרשורת נסמרות להוציא הלכה על ידן כמו שאמרנו
למעלה כאורה ד', הנה פרה ודאי כל עיקר זרה הלמוד אינו אלא
אסמכרחא, כמ"ש הר"ן בפירושו על הרי"ף שם, כיון דכל סדר חפלה
גופא דרבנן. ולא די שהמשניות והגמרורת שרתקו ולא רמזו אף שמץ

דבר שנשים אינן בכלל עשרה, .אלא גם בכל הפוסקים הראשונים
שהביאו הדין דכל דבר שבקדושה צריך להיות בעשרה אין אף אחד
שהוציא נשים מן הכלל, ורק הש"ע לבד הוא הראשון שהזכיר בא"ח
ראש סי' נ"ה שהעשרה צריכים להיות זכרים*) • נחזה נא בספרו
הגדול בית יוסף מאין הוציא כן, ונראה בסעט עיון, כי העמודים
אשר עליהם נשען בזה, עמודי ענן הם, רוח ישאם ואינם •

ז • פה בסי' נ"ה הביא הב"י דברי המרדכי בשם ר' שמחה
ראשה מצטרפרה ל'מנין עשרה ודהה אורו דנהגו העולם שלא
לצרף אשה כלל • מי שיש לו עין לראות יכיר, כי המנהג משענת
קנה רצוץ ויסוד רעוע לבנות הלכה עליו, ובענינינו בפרט נקל מאד
להציץ בין חרכי הזמנים ולראות איך נשתרבב זה המנהג בטעות,
כאשר אראה להלאה באורח ט' וע"י' במס' סופרים פי'ד סוף הלכה
י'ח: מנהג שאין לו ראייה מן החורה אינו אלא כטועה
בשקול הדעת" • וראה נ"כ דברי הרמב"ם בפירוש המשנה נטין
נ'ט א' המדברת מהדברים שחתנו מפני דרכי השלום, איך הרהמרמר
על המנהגים אשר אין להם שרש בש"ס •

שוב בב"י סי' קצ"ט וכב"מ פ"ה מהלכות ברכות ה"א ביאר דברי
הרמב"ם שהביא שם דברי המשנה (ברכות מ"ה א'), דנשים אין
מזמנין עליהן, ורבכרי הברייהא (שם ע"ב) דנשים מזמנות לעצמן,
ורהוסיף מעצמו „וכלבד שלא יזמנו בשם" על נקל באמרו:
„והטעם שאין מזמנין בשם משום דהוה דבר שבקדושה וכל דבר
שבקדושה לא יהא אלא ביוד אנשים גדולים ובני חורין" ולו יהי
שפירושו נכון כדעת הרמב"ם, הנה הרמב"ם לטעמיה אזיל בפ"א
מהל' ת"ח הנ"ל שנשים עני הרעת ולכן אין כבוד שמים בסקהלרן
ובאשר שכבר הראינו למעלה באות ר' שאין הדין עם הרמב"ם בזה
ושהש"ם מתנגד לדעה הזאת, נדחה מהלכרה ולא נאבה ולא נשמע
אליו • אבל באמת נראה בעיני ברור שאין הרמב"ם נחכוון כלל לדעת
הב"י, ואלו כן מדוע השמיט הרמב"ם דבר זה בפ"ח מהל' רהפלה כי
שם מקומו, שם העריך וסדר כל דיני דבר שבקדושה ושצריך עשרה
ולא רמז דבר או חצי דבר מזה שאין נשים בכלל העשרה, אע"פי
שבאר שם הל' ר' בפה מלא, שהעשרה צריכים להיות גדולים

<hr>

*) ובראם סי' קמ"ג בעל הט"ע שכח דעת עצמו וכתמך אחר הפוסקים
שקדמוה וכתב: „אין קורין בתורה בפחות מיוד גדולים בני חורין" ולא
הזכיר זכרים.

זכני חורין, ומה נקל מאד היה לו ׳להוסיף מלה אחת „וזכרים"
ולא עשה, ופרה, ופרה, אצל׳ ׳זמן, רק בכזור אחר מן הדכרים הצריכים
להיזת בעשרה, הלהו בין השטים כל׳שון סרהום והתום? הזה דלה׳
של העורך הנדול רבינו משה? אבל׳ באמרת טעם ה׳מב׳ם שנשים
אין סזמנורה כשם פשוט מאד מדאמרו ברכות שם „והא מאה נשי
כתרי גברי דמיין" ופירש הרמכ׳ם שם ״כפי׳רשי שם „כתרי גכר׳
לענין חובה שאין חיבורת לזמן" וכ׳עבור שרה׳זמור חשב מאה נשים
לענין זמן כהרי גברי, פשיטא נ״כ שאין מזמנוח בשם שצריך עשרה,
אבל׳ בתפלה וקדיש וקדושה שנשים חיבורה בהן ולא נאמר ולא
שייך שם לאמר: מאה נשי כתרי נכרי דמיין, דעת הרמכ׳ם נ״כ
שנשים יצטרפו לסניך עשרה. הן אמרת שהרהוס׳ שם ד״ה והוא כו׳
הביאו דעה ראשוננה שפירשה מאה נשי כהרי נברי „לענין קבוץ
תפלה ולעניך כל׳ דבר שבעשרה" נגד דעה רש׳י, אכל׳ במעט עיץ
נמצא כי דעת זו דחויה מרוב הפוסקים ומהרהוס׳ עצמם שם ד״ה
שאני הרהם, וערכין נ׳ א׳ ד״ה מזמנורה לעצמן, דמפרשי הכריירתא
„נשים מזמנורה לעצמן": רשורה ולא חובה, ועל׳ כרתך הוצאו זה
מלשיץ הרהזלמוד הנ״ל „והא מאה נשי כתרי נכרי דמיין" פירשו זה
כדעת רש׳י, ואל׳ו פרשו הלשון הזה כדיעה הא׳ כרהוס׳ הנ״ל דמאה
נשו כתרי נכרי לכל׳ דבר שבקרושה לא הי׳ להם סמך כלל׳: לפרש
מאמר הבריירתא „נשים מזמנות לעצמן" שיהי׳ רשורה ולא חובה, וזה
פשוט וכרור למעיין בסונירא שם, ורעת הרהוס׳ הא׳ הוו נדחה א׳כ
מהלכה. והש״ע עצמו שפסק בסי׳ קצ״ט סעיף ז׳ דנשים מזמנוח לעצמן
רשוה סהר בזה דעת עצמו בראש סי׳ נ״ה דנשים אינן בכלל׳ עשרה
לכל׳ דבר שבקרושה והרב כ״י ימחול׳ לי, כי לא עיין וברר הלכה זו
בכל׳ הצורך.

ח.   ואל׳ רהשיבני לשטרת רש׳י ורוכ הפוסקים מדוע באמרת
נשים מזמנוח רק רשות ולא חובה זכה אם הנשים לתפלה ולקדושה בכלל׳
עדה ועשרה הן? כי לפי דבריך אוסיף שאלה על שאלרהך: מדוע לא
יזמנו לפחות בשלש מצד החוב, כי הלא לא צריך בזה עדה ועשרה?
אמנם אמרה הדכר, שהשאלה, שהשאלה, אם הזמן לנשים רשורח או חובה,
אין לה המשך וענין כלל׳ אל השאלה שלנו, אם נשים בכלל׳ עדה
ועשרה או לו, וההעם האמרהי שהומן אצל׳ם רק רשורה הוא בעכור
שאין דרכן לקבוע בסעורה ולומן ולהכין עצמן כרהסידוח על השלהן,
כמו האנשים, רק ילכו ויכואו לראורח עניני הביח, ולכך אין חונרה
להן לישב ולהמחין עד שינרכו כהם׳ז בהזורה, רק חבירך כל׳ אחת
אם חרצה ורהעזוב השלהן בעכור עסקי הביח המוטלים עליה, והכל׳

להקל הטורח מעל שכמן, לא לחשבון פחותי הערך· ומה שלא
יצטרפו נשים עם אנשים לזמן עשרה ולברך ברכת הזמון בשם אם
ירצו לזמן, נ"כ אין לו ענין כלל לשאלתנו, אם נשים בכלל עדה,
כי גם לזמן בג' לא יצטרפו נשים עם אנשים, והטעם כתב רש"י
בערכין שם בעבור שהנשים לא יאמרו ברית בברכת הארץ, ולי
נראה שאין הרין עם רש"י כזה, שהרי כברכות כ' ב' ס"ל לגברא,
שאם נשים חייבות כבהמ"ז מה"ת יכלו להוציא אף אנשים ידי חובתם·
אע"פי שהן לא יאמרו ברית, ואם יוציאו אנשים י"ח, איך יהכן שלא
יצטרפו לזמן, אבל הטעם פשוט בעיני, שאף אם חייבות הנשים
בכהמ"ז מה"ת, אין חוכרה להן לזמן, בעבור עול הבית כנ"ל, ובכלל
זה נ"כ לא יוכלו להצטרף עם אנשים אל הזמן אף אם ירצו, כי לא
יצטרפו רק בעלי חובה, וככר נ"כ הר"ן בפירושו להרי"ף על המשנה
במגילה י"ט ב' הכל כשרין כו' הציב סברא זו הנכונה, שאם נשים
מוציאות אנשים בשום דבר פשיטא שיצטרפו נ"כ למנין עשרה אצל
זה הרבר· ומטעם זה פסק הר"ן שם שנשים סצטרפוה לקריאת
המגלה בעשרה, וקושירו שם מדוע לא חיישינן לפריצוה כמו
בכ"הזמן, אשר יישב רק כרוחק עצום, אינה קושיא כלל, כי לא
נחשדו ישראל על הפריצות, וכבהמ"ז דחחשש רק על העברים
שיפרצו פרץ, וכבר הבין ורמז זה הטיב הכ"ם בפ"ה מ"ל" ברכות
ה"ו ע"ש·

פ· ומעתה לפי כל האמור, אנחנו לא נרע כאמת אף
שמץ טעם וסברא, מדוע נפסל נשים להכנס רוך עדה קרושה
ולהצטרף ל"זמן עשרה לרתפלה ולכל דבר שבקרושה, זולת ברכת
המזון· חזרנו על כל המקומות בש"ם המדברים מענינים אלה ולא
מצאנו דבר או חצי דבר החזיק ידי המנרג הזה· אם אולי בעבור
קריאת שמע, אשר נקבע מקומו תוך סדר הרתפלה ונשים פטורות
ממנה? איה איפוא שמעגו שק"ש צריך להיוח בעשרה? רק פורסין
על שמע שמעגו (מגילה כ"נ כ') הרה לכל הרעורה בעבור קריש,
וברכו או עניה אמן שהם דברים שבקרושה, ורבר זה בכלל רפלה
שנשים חיבורה בה, ולא בכלל ק"ש· ואם אולי מפני ימי קריאת
הרחורה ובעבור שנשים פטורות מח"ת? כבר הוכחנו שנשים היבות
בלמוד ידיעה המצוה בלי שום חולק, וככר נפסק הרין נ"כ (ש"ע א"ח
סי' מ"ו) שנשים מברכוה ברכת התורה מטעם שהייבוה בלמוד המצות
שלהן· וכמס' סופרים פי"ה הל' ד' (הביאו המ"א כסי' רפ"ב ס"ק ו'),
נאמר בהריא שנשים חייבוה קריאה ס"ת כמו האנשים· וסצאתי
סמך יוחר לזה בטס' סופרים פ"א הי"ג שכתב: „ספר חורה שכרחכו

צדוקי או מסור או גר או עבד או שוטה או קטן אל יקרא בו, זה
הכלל כל הכוהבו מוציא את הרבים ידי הובחם" • הנה לא זכר אשה
בכלל הפסולים לכהיבת ס"ח, ודאי בעבור שלא שיך אליה הכלל
האמור, כי היא יכולה אפילו להוציא רבים ידי חובתן בקריאת התורה
וכגיטין ס"ה ב' שהחשב רב המנונא אף אשה בתוך הפסולים לכהיבת
ס"ח, באמת נהן טעם אחר ע"ש • והנה לפניך הלכה ברורה בגמ' דמגילה
כ"ג א', הובאה בש"ע א"ח סי' קפ"ב ג', הכל עולין למנין ז' (לקרות
בהורה), אפי' אשה, ורק משום כבוד הצבור אמרו אשה לא הקרא
בהורה, כי בימיהם הקרואים לתורה, הן הם הקוראים בהורה, ואשה לא
חשמיע קולה כצבור, משום צניעוהא• אם כן איפה, מדוע לא הצטרף לעשרה?

ואם באנו לחקור אחר המנהג, שהוא באמת בכל הפוצות
ישראל, שלא לצרף נשים למנין עשרה, מצאנו יסודו נגלה מאד
באפן בנין בהי כנסיוה הישנים, שהיהרה בהם עורת נשים נפרדה
ונבדלה מב'הכ של אנשים על ידי חומה גבוה ובצורה כל כך,
שכהין מפסיקה ושאפילו אם היו אנשים גדולים ובני חורין בעורת
נשים לא יוכלו להצטרף עם אוהן שכבית כנסת האנשים למנין עשרה
(עיי' ש"ע א"ח סי' נ"ה סעי' י"ג ולהלאה), ומזה נשהרבב הטעות וחשבו
העם שנשים פסולוה להצטרף לעולם• אבל לפי בנין בהי כנסיות
החדשים, צשר בהם מעמר הנשים לא נפסק ע"י מחיצה המפרדת
החבורה ומבטלה הצרוף, או בקבוץ לחפלה צבור בכירה, אין דין ואין
דה להוציא נשים מכלל מנין עשרה, כאשר הראיתי וברריתי בעה"י. —

וללנו המו"ים בעם, ראוי לדעת ולהודיע, כי לא נקברה החכמה
בעהותי קדם, ובקרת האמת לא ברהה סני רהבל• כאשר קרוב ה'
לכל קוראיו באמת, כן מרה האכה, חותמו של הקב"ה, לא בשמים
ולא מעבר לים היא, רק בקרבנו השכון, בלבנו ובכליוהנו, כל
מבקשיה ימצאונה, ויגעתי ומצאתי לעולם האמין• אף לנו נהן אלהים
חלק ונחלה בהורה וחכמה ורוח משפט להבדיל בין האמת והשקר;
אף אוהנו העמיד על משמרתו, לעורר הלבבות ולוכך המחשבות, למען
לא יכול הינם כסנהגים בל ידעום ובמצות אנשים מלומדה והי האמת
נעררת• העירו והקיצו ישבי על מדין הסירו הרדמת ההרגל מקרבכם
ומסוה היראה מפני עמי הארצות מעל פניכם, ואמרו לעם ה': הנה
כלכם, כעם ככהן, כנשים כאנשים, גאולי ה', ובכלכם בהר אל לבנוח
עמודי עולם, הורה ועבודה וגמ"ח! „כהדי ככשי דרחמנא לימה לך
מאי רמפקדה איבעי לך למעבד"!

CONTRIBUTORS

Samuel Adler (1809-1901) was rabbi in Alzey (Germany) and Temple Emanu-El in New York. An active participant in the rabbinic conferences in Brunswick, Frankfurt, Breslau, and Philadelphia, he fought vigorously for civil rights for Jews in Germany before emigrating to the United States in 1857. He was elected as honorary president of the Central Conference of American Rabbis at its founding meeting in 1889. His collected papers were published as *Kobetz al Yad* (1886).

Walter Jacob is President of the Abraham Geiger College in Berlin/Potsdam; Senior Scholar of Rodef Shalom Congregation, Pittsburgh, Pennsylvania; President of the Freehof Institute of Progressive *Halakhah* and the Associated American Jewish Museums. Author, editor, or translator of thirty-eight books including *Christianity through Jewish Eyes* (1974), *American Reform Responsa* (1983), *The Pittsburgh Platform in Retrospect* (1985), *Liberal Judaism and Halakhah* (1988), *The Second Book of the Bible: Exodus Interpreted by Benno Jacob* (1992), *Die Exegese hat das erste Wort* (2002), *Pursuing Peace Across the Alleghenies* (2005), *Hesed and Tzedakah - From the Bible to Modernity (*2006*), Napoleon's Influence on Jewish Law (2008)*.

Peter Knobel is President of the Central Conference of American Rabbi, chair of its Liturgy Committee, and rabbi of Beth Emet, Evanston, Illinois. He is past president of the Chicago Board of Rabbis. He is the author of papers on assisted suicide, homosexuality, and spirituality and is editor of *Gates of the Season* (1983), *Duties of the Soul: The Role of Commandments in Liberal Judaism* (1999), and *Mishkan Tefillah (2007)*, the new American Reform prayer book.

Leonard Kravitz is professor of Midrash and Homiletics at the Hebrew Union College– Jewish Institute of Religion in New York. He has served on the Medical Ethics Committee of the New York Federation of Philanthropies. Author of *The Esoteric Meaning of Maimonides' Guide for the Perplexed* (1988); *Shemona Perakim: Treatise on the Soul* (1996); *Kohelet: A Modern Commentary on Ecclesiastes* (2000)*; Mishlei, A Modern Commentary on Proverbs* (2002)*; Pirke Avot: A Modern Commentary on Jewish Ethics* (2005)*; Ruth: A Modern Commentary*.

Ruth Langer is Associate Professor of Jewish Studies in the Theology Department at Boston College and Associate Director of its Center for Christian-Jewish Learning. She received her Ph.D. in 1994 and her rabbinic ordination in 1986, both from Hebrew Union College–Jewish Institute of Religion in Cincinnati. Her research focuses on Jewish liturgy and Jewish–Christian relations. Along with numerous monographs, her books include *To Worship God Properly: Tensions between Liturgical Custom and Halakhah in Judaism*, Cincinnati (1998); *Liturgy in the Life of the Synagogue: Studies in the History of Jewish Prayer*, ed. Ruth Langer and Steven Fine, Winona Lake, Indiana (2005).